The Legend of Zelda and Theology

Edited by

Jonathan L. Walls

Gray Matter Books
www.graymatterbooks.com

© 2011 Jonathan L. Walls

Edited by Joan Sanford
         Emily Walls

All rights reserved. No portion of this book may be reproduced, stored in a retrieval system, or transmitted in any form by any means including but not limited to electronic, mechanical, photocopy, recording, scanning or other except for brief quotations in critical reviews or articles, without the prior written permission of the publisher.

Published in U.S.A.

ISBN 978-0984779000

Gray Matter Books titles may be purchased in bulk at wholesale discounts. Please contact info@graymatterbooks.com for additional information.

▲ CASUAL
▲▲ NORMAL
△ ADVANCED

CHOOSE YOUR DIFFICULTY LEVEL

While all of our chapters explore meaningful, theological ideas, some are denser and more in depth in their approach, while others are more topical and touch multiple bases. I am confident that readers of all experience levels will find every chapter rewarding and insightful, and hopefully these difficulty indicators will help you approach this book in the way that fits you best.

	Introduction	11
▲	Linking the Landscapes of Twilight Princess and Christian Theology **Kyle Blanchette**	17
▲▲	Trouble in the Golden Realm: Ganondorf and Hyrule's Problem of Evil in Ocarina of Time **Jonathan L. Walls**	31
▲▲	The Birth of Gaming from the Spirit of Fantasy: Video Games as Secondary Worlds with Special Reference to The Legend of Zelda and J. R. R. Tolkien **Philip Tallon**	47
△	Freedom versus Destiny: A Hero's Call **Josh and Rachel Rasmussen**	71
▲▲	The Mediation of Transcendence within The Legend of Zelda: The Wind Waker **Mark Hayse**	83

Take Your Time, Hurry Up, The Choice is Yours: Death and the Afterlife in The Legend of Zelda: Majora's Mask
Josh Corman   97

On Hylian Virtues: Aristotle, Aquinas and the Hylian Cosmogenesis
Justus Hunter   109

High Rule? Vintage Virtue in The Legend of Zelda
Benjamin B. DeVan   125

Portals, Prophecy and Cuccos: Considerations of Power in A Link to the Past
Jeremy Smith   143

The Necessity of the Triforce in the Defeat of Ganon
D.M. Burke   155

Bios   171

To my Dad.
Finally I get to dedicate one to you. May this inspire you to pick up the controller and see the world through Link's eyes for yourself.

A WORD OF THANKS

Special thanks to my dad for insights, suggestions, proofreading and encouragement. Quite literally, this book could not have been done without you. Thanks to my mom for buying me my first copy of Zelda. Thanks to David Baggett, Elizabeth Glass-Turner, and Luke Van Horn for additional insights and opinions. Thanks, as always, to my wife Emily for proofreading my contributions, for valuable opinions and for being so attractive.

Introduction

    I've been a video gamer all my life. The original Nintendo Entertainment System and I were born the same year (it was released in America two years later). Over the years, I spent countless hours absorbed in and enamored with many classic game franchises in their infancy such as *Mario, Star Fox, Street Fighter* and *Teenage Mutant Ninja Turtles*, to name just a few. As a gamer, I was insatiable. Video games provided immersion, fantasy, challenge and, most importantly, *fun*.

    Little did I know as a child, however, the untapped adventures that still lay beyond my limited gaming horizons. This was long before the Internet and I hadn't a concept of researching and educating myself on the best games available, like I do now. I simply played what I had access to and, for one reason or another, I'd never been exposed firsthand to Shigeru Miyamoto's, *The Legend of Zelda*. I didn't have a clue that a series of games so rich in theme, adventure, lively characters and puzzle solving existed.

    In 1986 and 1987, *The Legend of Zelda* was released in Japan and America/Europe, respectively, to an unknowing generation of gamers. Woefully ignorant and unprepared for the bomb that was about to be dropped on their fledgling, isolated community, gamers could not have known the Beatles-esque impact this new game would have. To put it bluntly, everything changed.

    The level of interactive adventure, exploration, immersion and storytelling *The Legend of Zelda* brought to television screens across the world was unheard of and it planted an integral seed in the garden that one day would grow into the diverse gaming landscape we know today. Far from stopping there, *The Legend of Zelda* series has continued to release top-shelf games adored by critics and fans alike.

    My first real encounter with *Zelda* was at an early age when the series itself was relatively young. While at a friend's house, I saw in his collection a Super Nintendo game called, *The Legend of Zelda: A Link to the Past.* I had heard of *Zelda* in passing, and I think I even knew that there was some protagonist named Link, so I got the pun. Upon further inspection, I saw that the face of the game cartridge was crudely altered so that the words *The Legend of Zelda* had been crossed out with a blue pen and the name "Jesus" written instead. Likely, one or both of his parents were behind this and now my poor friend's game cartridge (sort of) read, *Jesus: A Link to the Past.* Amusing, perhaps, but this did little to pique my interest in the game.

My love for *Zelda* began a few years later with the release of *The Legend of Zelda: The Ocarina of Time* (the next installment in the series) in 1998. If *The Legend of Zelda* is The Beatles of video games, then this installment was *Sergeant Pepper's.* I received the game and a Nintendo 64 unexpectedly for Christmas. I immediately began to devour this new and unprecedented treat.

The game changed my life.

Anyone who played this masterpiece when it came out will know of what I speak. Hyrule was positively *massive.* I could go anywhere I wanted and explore at my own pace. I wasn't just playing a game, I was living out an ancient mythology, meeting new and unfamiliar people, discovering lost lands, solving riddles, avoiding traps and wiping out evil. When I finally finished the game, I experienced true, forceful nostalgia which, quite frankly, took me by surprise. It wasn't merely that I had never felt anything like that from a video game before; it was that it kicked in before the credits even rolled. That meant this wasn't misplaced nostalgia for the period of my life connected with playing the game (although that is a powerful emotion experienced by many *Zelda* players). No, this was nostalgia for *the game itself:* for Hyrule, for Lake Hylia, for the Temples, villages, caves and forests *themselves.* I had no idea a game was capable of such potency and it stirred up new longings in my heart.

C.S. Lewis said, "I think that all things, in their way, reflect heavenly truth, the imagination not least."[1] Through this finely

---

1 C.S Lewis, *Surprised by Joy* (Harcourt, Inc. New York), 167

Introduction

articulated point, which (to generalize) is based on the belief that *all good things come from God,* Lewis maintained that all great myths and religions hold elements of truth in them, and that all this partial truth finally was completed and perfected in the ultimate, historically true myth, the story of Christ.

Can you find elements of truth in your favorite books, films, music and games? Can one find truth in the works of Lennon and Cobain? How about in Tyler Durden or in the Cantina on Mos Eisley? Dante, Steinbeck or Harry Potter? I think so. This isn't to say that everything is true, but that truth appears in a lot of places we may not first suspect.

Before diving into the chapters of this book, let us clearly state what this book is, and is not, trying to accomplish. For fans of the *Zelda* series, hopefully, this will be a reminder of why you so adore these marvelous games. Perhaps you will experience the same sort of nostalgia I mentioned as you read about and relive the priceless gaming moments mentioned in these chapters. Maybe seeing the rich *Zelda* mythology from a different angle will help you appreciate it in a fresh way. For any of you who are not familiar with the *Zelda* series, maybe this book will help you understand why we love it.

Whether you hold a Christian worldview or not, it is our intention that these articles clarify and provide you with a better understanding of *why* Christians believe what we believe. Christianity is a faith of the heart *and* the head. While the Bible repeatedly calls us to delight in the beauty of creation, Christ also calls for us to be as *cunning as serpents.*[2] Anyone who has played a *Zelda* game knows that the *Zelda* universe is no different. While you bask in sweeping music, enchanted worlds and visual art direction to rival any animated film, you are also required to use your brain to track down elusive items and solve mysteries.

Please understand, however, that none of us claim to have found the intended meaning behind the *Zelda* mythology's symbolism

---

2   Matthew 10:16

when we relate it to Christianity. A very astute theological thinker and friend warned me of the error of superimposing Christian beliefs onto games that very well may have been made *without* Christian beliefs in mind. Let me assure you, we intend no superimposing. Attempting to find an intentional and exclusive allegorical connection between *Zelda* mythology and Christian theology would be utterly erroneous and a dead end.

So when we claim, for example, that *Majora's Mask*, in some ways, reflects parallels to Christian beliefs about the soul, or that *A Link to the Past* may illuminate the teachings of St. Augustine, we do not claim that these things are what the *Zelda* games are *about,* at least in any intentional or deliberate sense. What we do intend, however, is to look at Zelda through the lens of Christianity and see what shape it begins to take from that point of view.

Another important note before we dive in: Please bear in mind the monumental and, ultimately, impossible task that is encapsulating these complex and layered topics of theology into a roughly 4,000 word essay. It simply can't be done. As such, there are apparent flaws, reasonable objections and potential problems to accompany every purported theology and theory you will find within our book. We simply don't have time or space to address them all. The point of these articles is not to give you lock down, airtight, fully fleshed out theses and defenses of these varying beliefs and ideas. It is, rather, to introduce, re-examine and possibly even present in a new fashion these time-tested viewpoints and philosophies. Pay attention to the sources and footnotes. They are there to provide you with options for further, deeper studies, for and against the things we suggest to you.

Think again of my friend's game cartridge. The perpetrator of this defacing could never have known all those years ago what a perfect anecdote he or she was setting up for this book. As lame as that was for my friend's parent to do, Jesus *is* The Ultimate Link to the Past. As Christians, we believe that all truth, beauty and goodness point back to their source: God, the Creator. Remember, this book isn't

Introduction

about trying to speculate or claim to know what Shigeru Miyamoto or anyone else truly believes. It is not about trying to shoehorn *Zelda* into an exclusively Christian mold or make it something it is not. It *is*, however, about bringing our point of view to the table alongside Nintendo's brilliantly crafted mythology. Because *Zelda*, like all of our greatest fairy tales, legends and myths, presents that elusive and exclusive kind of enlightenment that only the fantastic can provide.

-Jonathan L. Walls

Linking the Landscapes of Twilight Princess and Christian Theology

Kyle Blanchette

A Link to the Truth

In the very first cinematic cutscene of *The Legend of Zelda: Twilight Princess*, we hear of "lingering regrets of spirits who have left our world." When dusk falls, a strange sadness can be felt because, as they say, dusk is the only time our world intersects with "theirs." Link displays his usual quiet, yet attentive, disposition as the unnamed Postman pensively reflects upon what we later find out is the Twilight Realm. These spirits who have left Hyrule are not, however, the souls of those who have died, which is what most players, especially Christians, are likely to assume at the outset of *Twilight Princess*. What is more, Midna, the imp-like Twilight creature who guides Link throughout the story, is clear that the Twili are not an evil people; they are simply different, and they are needed in order to strike a harmonious balance between light and darkness. This is a divergence from the common Christian symbolism of darkness as evil and light as good, which are themes found throughout the Bible, especially in Johannine literature;[1] instead, in the *Twilight Princess* worldview, darkness is not necessarily correlated with evil, just as light is not necessarily correlated with good.

Given that *Twilight Princess* is not an explicitly Christian video game, such obvious differences between the Christian understanding of reality and the *Zelda* worldview should not be surprising. But differences aside, if one looks carefully enough, one can catch glimpses of implicit Christian truth suffused throughout the *Twilight Princess* narrative and world structure. The Christian worldview actually provides believers with a powerful theological rationale for making certain compelling

---

1 E.g. John 1:5, 3:19, 8:12; 1 John 1:5, 2:9.

connections between Christian teaching and the manifold productions of human creativity, including video games. Christian thinkers spanning the timeline of church history, from Justin Martyr[2] to C.S. Lewis[3], have held that it is only natural to expect that God has spun threads of Christian truth into the various fabrics that make up all of creation. Apart from the explicit revelation given by God through the people of Israel and the life, death and resurrection of Jesus Christ, these thinkers believe that God also speaks implicitly through conscience, the general religious yearnings of humanity and the inspired products of human imagination, albeit in a more incomplete, inchoate manner.[4] From a Christian perspective, God is calling the world back into loving relationship with Himself, and He will use any means possible to accomplish this goal, including, believe it or not, when you boot up your Nintendo Wii.

Both the *Zelda* saga, in general, and *Twilight Princess* entry, in particular, contain themes that are deeply evocative of central Christian convictions about the nature of God and the nature of reality. Rather than explore in detail how *Twilight Princess* illuminates one particular Christian teaching, let us take a step back and survey the broad

---

2 Martyr, Justin. *Apology. Documents of the Christian Church*. Ed. Henry Bettenson. 2nd ed. New York: Oxford University Press, 1963. 5. Martyr argues that whenever philosophers arrive at truth, they are encountering seeds of the Word, which is a title, found also in John 1:1, for the second person of the Trinity, the Christian Godhead (comprised of three persons in one nature – Father, Son and Holy Spirit).

3 Lewis, C.S. *Mere Christianity*. New York: HarperCollins, 1996. 50-51. Lewis calls the religious graspings of humankind "good dreams."

4 A minority of Christian thinkers throughout the history of the church have been radically exclusivist in their understanding of the accessibility of genuine spiritual truth, in that they seem to deny any valid spiritual insight to those outside the reach of special revelation. One notable example is Tertullian, whose opposition to spiritual truth outside of explicit Christian revelation is apparent in his famous phrase, "What has Jerusalem to do with Athens, the Church with the Academy, the Christian with the heretic?" See Tertullian. *The Prescriptions Against the Heretics. Readings in Christian Thought*. Ed. Hugh T. Kerr. 2nd ed. Nashville: Abingdon Press, 1990. 40.

metaphysical landscapes of *Twilight Princess* and Christianity. When we widen our vision to get a panoramic shot, three key themes stretch across the horizons of both pictures: creation and fall, the inherent relationality of both universes and the nature of evil and the reality of redemption.

In the Beginning

We have seen that the Twili are not necessarily evil and that the Twilight Realm is not the realm of the dead. How, then, did the Twilight Realm come to be? In order to answer that question, the *Twilight Princess* narrative takes us all the way back to the beginning; indeed, we are treated to a veritable story of origins, a "genesis" of how the current world came to be. Lanayru, one of the Light Spirits whom Link restores in the course of the story, tells us that "when all was chaos, the goddesses descended and gave order and life to the world." The language used here is strikingly reminiscent of Genesis 1:2, which states, "Now the earth was formless and void, darkness was over the surface of the deep, and the Spirit of God hovered over the waters. And God said, 'Let there be light,' and there was light." Lanayru does not tell us how this chaotic state of affairs itself came to be, but we are told that, just as on the Christian picture, the deities imposed order upon the chaos and brought life into being. Moreover, in both narratives, the respective deities move in close proximity to the locus of divine activity, whether that is depicted in terms of "descending" in the case of *Twilight Princess*, or "hovering" in the case of Biblical teaching.[5]

Giving order and life to the world, the goddesses distributed power equally among those who live in the light, after which they returned to the heavens. This theme of equality mirrors what we find in Genesis 1:27 about men and women created equally in the image of God: "So God created mankind in His image, in the image of God He created

---

5   Genesis 1:2

them; male and female He created them." Both of these narratives tap into the widespread and well-founded intuition that a certain sort of equality in terms of power, rights and the like is necessary to underwrite equal dignity and worth among persons, be they human or elf.[6] The land upon which the goddesses descended – the land that was the locus of the divine activity – came to be known as the Sacred Realm, which can be taken almost as the *Zelda* version of the Garden of Eden. "For ages," Lanayru informs us, "the people lived at ease, content in mind and body." In other words, this was a time of flourishing and happiness, which was the design of the goddesses, and is also the desire of the Christian God for all of His creatures. When things are operating as the benevolent, creative deities intended, all is well. Their order and design are aimed at the flourishing of their respective creations.

Let There Be Twilight

The "fall from grace," as it were, occurs as a result of the all-too-common desire for inordinate power and status, a theme that resonates deeply with Christian conceptions of evil. Once the news of the Sacred Realm spread through Hyrule, "interlopers" who excelled at magic arose from the people of the light and they attempted to establish dominion over the Sacred Realm using powerful sorcery. It was then that the goddesses ordered the Light Spirits to intervene and they sealed away the magic used by the interlopers. This ancient magic is sealed away in the Fused Shadows that Link and Midna are after for most of the story, a dark power that was never intended to be found again. After relating all

---

6   This is not to say that all asymmetrical relationships of power are inherently evil; fans of the *Zelda* series are likely to object strenuously to such a notion, given the noble status of Princess Zelda in the mythos! Note, too, that although God commissioned Adam and Eve to "fill the earth and subdue it" (Genesis 1:28), this is quite different from seeking out inordinate dominion. This mandate here is, like God, to bring order out of chaos, and exercise loving authority over the animal realm.

of this to Link and Midna, Lanayru then solemnly warns Link that "those who do not know the danger of wielding power will, before long, be ruled by it."

Lust for power and position are common themes of evil in the Christian story as well. Traditional Christian theology tells that although God created the world good, it is in many senses "fallen" as a result of the entrance of sin into the world. This fall includes angels, such as Satan, as well as those human beings who have followed the temptations of the Evil One into sin, from the first humans onward. Pride is usually featured centrally in theological accounts of these primordial sins: the Devil became jealous of God's position and Adam and Eve took it upon themselves to run their lives and decide what was best for them apart from God's loving guidance, an act represented by eating of the tree of good and evil.[7] When creatures sinfully grasp for the rightful power and position of God, this naturally leads to power struggles among creatures as well, as they all try to be "on top" in terms of power, possessions or whatever else they choose to turn into a competition. Instead of being defined by mutual love and care, they become defined *over against* one another in a zero-sum game of survival.

A clear biblical example of such a broken power relationship can be found in Genesis 3:16, in which we read the following consequence of human sin on gender relationships: "Your desire will be for your husband, and he will rule over you." And although "with great power comes great responsibility" has become a relatively hackneyed platitude since the advent of the *Spider-Man* film series, this, nevertheless, rings true in both the *Zelda* mythos and the Christian worldview. Jesus expressed this basic point when He said, "To whom much is given, much is required."[8] One must be prepared to use great power, lest one become ruled by that power through its misuse. Just as "He who sins is a slave to sin," as Jesus put it, those who, in the *Twilight Princess* mythos, wield the

---

7   Genesis 2-3.
8   Luke 12:48.

Fused Shadows without due respect will become their slave."

As the *Twilight Princess* narrative progresses, it becomes clear that the magic-wielding interlopers were banished to the Twilight Realm by the goddesses. The Twilight Realm, then, seems to be a later creation by the goddesses, intended as a place of banishment for the power-hungry interlopers. Whereas God ejects the primeval pair out of the Garden of Eden and places a cherubim in its entrance to prevent their reentry,[9] the goddesses in Hyrule prevent the offending group from ever taking over the Sacred Realm by removing them permanently to another realm. Since then, a whole tribe of shadow people, the Twili, have descended from these original rebels. Midna, eventually, informs us that she, too, is a descendent of these ancient sorcerers.

Though the Twilight Realm was originally made for the ignoble, the race of Twili people that grew forth from that group is not necessarily evil. Before one of the main villains of the story, Zant, comes on the scene, Midna tells us that there is a "serene beauty" to the Twilight Realm that can be seen when the sun goes down in the light world: "bathed in that light [Twilight], all people were pure and gentle." Zelda states that the important thing is for the two dichotomous worlds to remain *balanced*. The darkness cannot encroach upon the light, and vice versa. God, too, is "not a God of disorder, but of peace," creating everything with an aim toward harmony, balance and order.[10] In a real sense, certain realms also "emerge" in the Christian metaphysical landscape as they become needed; meaning, the choices of humans and other free beings "spill over" into the next life. Those who are stubbornly and irremediably unrepentant create the need for separation and the punishment of hell. The fact that many, perhaps most, faithful believers die without reaching perfection in Christlikeness, according to some Christians, calls out for purgatory.[11] Of course, both hell and purgatory

---

9   Genesis 3:24.
10 1 Corinthians 14:33.
11 Some Christians argue that any remaining moral imperfections in believers at death are dealt with instantaneously by God, leaving no need for

only come about as a result of human sin, but heaven is God's hope and desire for all His free creatures.

Relationality Reigns

There is no direct or complete parallel to the Twilight Realm in the Christian worldview, but the way in which it functions in relationship to the light world is one of the symbols in *Twilight Princess* that resembles the profoundly relational nature of the Christian worldview. Christians have had differing views on the relationships between inhabitants of heaven, earth and purgatory (for those Christians who affirm purgatory),[12] but at the very least, all Christians believe that angelic and spiritual beings frequently interact with our world. The theme of spiritual warfare plays a significant role in the biblical worldview, and the biblical tradition has countless examples of angels interfering in human affairs, for good and for ill. In Ephesians 6:12, believers are told that their struggle is not against flesh and blood, but against, among other things, "the spiritual forces of evil in the heavenly realm." It is the angel Gabriel who foretells the imminent birth of Jesus Christ to the virgin Mary.[13] The Light Spirits of the *Zelda* universe function quite persuasively as the *Zelda* equivalent of angels, called as they are to do the bidding of the goddesses by protecting Hyrule, in general, and tracking down the interlopers, in particular.

In addition to this, since the beginning of the Christian movement, most Christians have conceived of some kind of relational connection between living and dead Christians via the communion of the saints. The most relevant Biblical passage on this point is Hebrews

---

purgatory. All Christians agree that there will be no sin in heaven.

12 A version of purgatory is officially affirmed by Roman Catholics, and many Eastern Orthodox theologians favor the doctrine. The general Protestant rejection of purgatory is tied up with the theological controversies surrounding the Reformation. See Walls, Jerry. *Heaven: The Logic of Eternal Joy*. New York: Oxford University Press, 2002. 52.

13 Luke 1:26-38.

11-12, which suggests that there is a "cloud of witnesses" that is, in a real sense, cheering us on in the journey that they themselves have successfully completed. In the *Twilight Princess* worldview, though those banished to the Twilight Realm were prohibited from returning to the light world, according to Midna, it was, nevertheless, the intention of the goddesses that the chosen one, Zelda, and the Twilight princess at some point meet. This is why they left one link between the light and the darkness, the Mirror of Twilight. Recall, too, that those in the light world can access a faint sense of the shadow realm at dusk, an indication that the two worlds "make an impression," so to speak, on one another. The very imagery of light and darkness is evocative of interdependence and relationality.

Some Christians have taken the relationship between the living and the dead a step further, arguing that those on earth can influence those in purgatory. Such Christians have typically thought it proper to pray for those going through the cleansing process in purgatory, and early Christians even practiced baptism (by proxy) for the dead. Of course, abuses surrounding purgatory eventually emerged and came to a fever pitch by the time of the Protestant Reformation. These abuses circled mostly around the buying and selling of indulgences, which is technical theological language for release from having to pay "temporal satisfaction" for one's sin.[14] In other words, some radical theologians were suggesting that even after forgiveness, we must in some sense incur, or pay for, the results of one's sins – and one could bypass this process by making a donation to the church. While some theologians still defend versions of a "satisfaction" model of purgatory, most feel that such a model undermines the work of Christ in bearing our sin. Thus, these theologians would opt for a model of purgatory that sees it simply as a place to finish one's process of spiritual formation into the likeness of Christ. In accordance with this model, it makes perfect theological sense to pray for such persons in hope that they grow closer to Christ,

---

14   Griffiths, Paul. "Purgatory." *The Oxford Handbook of Eschatology*. Ed. Jerry Walls. New York: Oxford University Press, 2008. 430-433.

even in the hereafter.

Now one might ask, why did the goddesses commission the Light Spirits to guard the ancient magic of the Fused Shadows? Why did they not take care of the matter themselves, a task they easily could have accomplished? Analogously, why does God often call lower creatures to do His bidding and will when He easily could accomplish what He desires directly? More radical still, why does God create free creatures capable of relationship and choice in the first place? A common Christian answer to consider is **the intrinsic goods that free will makes possible in created beings, such as authentic relationships, genuine love, and weighty virtue.**[15] John Wesley, founder of the Methodist movement, argued that the entire created order was made for relationships of various kinds, all the way down to the animals, such that each creature would be happy in the fulfillment of its own nature – provided that those who possess significant freedom use that freedom rightly.[16]

Most fundamentally, in both worldviews, the theme of interrelationship extends all the way up to the Godhead. The foundation and ontological starting point of the Christian faith is the doctrine of the Trinity, the Christian Godhead, which affirms that God is three persons in one nature/substance: Father, Son and Holy Spirit. These three persons exist in an eternal relationship of shared life, perfect love and interdependence. In the *Zelda* universe, we see what might be called a

---

15   Because God is the ultimate causal source of all things in Christian theology, He need not have the ability to choose evil in order to be able to love. Therefore, though God is impeccable according to Christian theology (He is necessarily good and cannot choose evil), there are no causal forces prior to Himself compelling Him to so choose, so He is still free enough to love genuinely. For created beings, however, unless we have the freedom to choose between good and evil, our choices would be causally determined by prior causes (ultimately, by God), thus vitiating our freedom and our ability to participate in genuine creaturely love. Therefore, creatures must have the ability to choose evil in order to be truly free and in order to truly love, though God need not have this ability.

16   Wesley, John. "Sermon 60, The General Deliverance." *Global Ministries: The United Methodist Church.* Ed. Sarah Anderson. < http://new.gbgm-umc.org/umhistory/wesley/sermons/60/> 14 November 2010.

refined polytheism of three goddesses. It is polytheistic because there are three distinct deities here, unlike the great monotheistic religions, and it is refined because it seems that these three goddesses are always in harmony with one another, having intentions that are both united and aimed at the good. Community, relationships and plurality are celebrated in the *Zelda* universe and the Christian worldview alike. By incorporating all of these elements, perhaps *Zelda* is implicitly pointing to the value and significance of free will, shared life and mutual relationships.

Trial by Twilight: Evil and Redemption

Any story worthy of the epithet "epic" has to feature some kind of battle between good and evil and *Twilight Princess* fits the bill. Christianity, of course, strongly affirms the reality of radical evil, although it is careful to situate it in proper relationship to the good. From Augustine of Hippo, to Thomas Aquinas, all the way to present day, Christians have generally conceived of evil as a perversion, or even a privation, of the good. Goodness, on the other hand, is fundamental, not derived, and ultimate; that is to say, it is rooted in the necessary nature of God Himself, and it does not depend upon anything else for its existence. One can even find some early Christian thinkers who say that evil does not have being, nor does it properly exist, since goodness and being are one and both flow from God. By this, early thinkers such as Aquinas did not mean to say that evil is not instantiated in the world – that it does not truly exist in our modern use of that term – but rather that evil does not fulfill a created thing's form or purpose.[17] The upshot of all of this is that although Christianity affirms the *dichotomy* of good and evil, it utterly rejects all *dualistic* understandings of good and evil that would put them on equal footing; goodness, flowing ultimately

---

17   Brown, Clare and Jerry Walls. "Annihilation: A Philosophical Dead End?" *The Problem of Hell: A Philosophical Anthology.* Ed. Joel Buenting. Burlington: Ashgate Publishing Company, 2010. 45-64.

from the Triune God, is simply greater in status and power than any form of evil ever could be. Evil is, by nature, parasitic.

Thematic overlap on this topic abounds. For instance, the player gets a vivid symbol of evil as a parasite in *Twilight Princess* when Link encounters multiple dark insects throughout the course of restoring the Light Spirits. The bugs must attach to the scattered light of the Light Spirits in order to manifest themselves in the light world. Not only does evil depend upon good, but in this case, darkness depends upon light.

The evil form of Twilight is often portrayed as violent and it is able to take possession of the noble tribe of the Gorons, a rock-eating, mountain-dwelling race in Hyrule, quickly transforming it into something quite unlike its original, benevolent form. In the same vein, the violent and transformative nature of demonic possession is frequently highlighted in the exorcisms of Jesus in the Gospel accounts. One particularly vivid example is found in Luke 8:27-29:

> When Jesus stepped ashore, he was met by a demon-possessed man from the town. For a long time this man had not worn clothes or lived in a house, but had lived in the tombs. When he saw Jesus, he cried out and fell at his feet, shouting at the top of his voice, 'What do you want with me, Jesus, Son of the Most High God? I beg you, don't torture me!' For Jesus had commanded the impure spirit to come out of the man. Many times it had seized him, and though he was chained hand and foot and kept under guard, he had broken his chains and had been driven by the demon into solitary places.

Biblical concepts related to dealing with evil, such as "cleansing" and "redemption," show up in *Twilight Princess* in relation to the land itself, which has become covered in twilight "like a shroud" due to Zant's evil actions. The Old Testament, in particular, speaks of a holy land and the cleansing of the land, although the New Testament reveals that these were merely physical types of the deeper realities of inward holiness and moral cleansing.[18] Even the concept of a "chosen one," or election, is present in both narratives, which is clearly election for the purpose of noble service in both instances.[19]

But what "screams Christian" more than anything else with reference to evil in *Twilight Princess,* perhaps, is the atonement language that Zelda imputes to Midna. When Link brings a seriously wounded Midna to Zelda, Zelda has this to say: "Midna, I now understand what you are. Despite your mortal injuries, you act in our stead. These dark times are the result of our deeds, yet it is you who have reaped the penalty." The crucial difference here, according to Christian theology, is that Christ had every intention of suffering for us from the beginning for the sake of our salvation; whereas, Midna began her cooperation with the light realm with a kind of resentful resignation, seeing it as little more than an expedient path of action to save her own realm. It was only after she became personally acquainted with the selfless acts of Zelda and Link that she began to see the worth of the light realm and desired to save it as well. Christ, of course, loved us and died for us "while we were yet sinners."[20] But what does Zelda mean? In what sense are the current dark times a result of the deeds of those in the light? This question takes us to the story of Ganondorf, who, as we would expect, plays a key role in this episode of the *Zelda* saga.

When Midna and Link finally reach the Mirror of Twilight in hopes of using it to cross into the Twilight Realm and defeat Zant, they find a group of sages guarding the mirror, which turns out to be broken. The sages explain that Zant broke the mirror, scattering the shards all over Hyrule. Only the true ruler of the Twili, they note, could ever utterly

---

18 Revelation 21:10.

19 In the Old Testament, God is clear that Israel has been chosen not primarily for its own sake, but rather to be a "light to the Gentiles" (Isaiah 42:6). In the New Testament, too, the church is chosen "in Christ" to be conformed to the image of Christ in service to the world (Ephesians 1:10-11; 1 Peter 1:2, 2:9).

20 Romans 5:8.

destroy it. It is revealed that the source of Zant's power is none other than Ganondorf, who the sages describe as a ruthless, magic-wielding bandit with an "abiding hatred and lust for power." About a century ago, Ganondorf attempted to take dominion over the Sacred Realm, but like most men who become drunk with power, he eventually became foolhardy. Once Ganondorf's hubris exposed him to capture, the sages tried to kill him with a sword made of light. But, as they put it, they "overestimated their ability as sages" in this attempt and Ganondorf was able to withstand their efforts to kill him. They, then, hastily banished him to the Twilight Realm as something of a last-ditch effort to deal with him after their efforts to kill him.[21] This was their error and Midna bore the consequences of it.

    Ganondorf got his strength to endure the efforts of the sages by drawing upon the bitterness of the ancient Twili rebels, whose anguish as a result of being cast aside by the gods gave him strength and awakened him. Even Midna seems to resent the people of the light at the outset due to past treatment by the goddesses. Recall that the entire history of the Twili and the Twilight Realm began on an evil and bitter note with the rise and banishment of the magic-wielding interlopers. This sour note was sustained all the way through to Ganondorf, who used this inspiration to create his own twisted counterpoint, resulting in an ever-growing dissonance of evil. This evil and bitter beginning of the Twili spawned even greater evil down the road and there seems to be no hope at stopping the downward spiral. In an ironic twist, the Twilight Realm, which was originally created as a way of dealing with evil, threatens to become the source of the light world's demise.

    But notice that although the history of the Twili people and the Twilight Realm begins with evil, banishment and bitterness, it eventually finds its way to goodness, reconciliation and peace. Midna realizes at the end that goddesses left the Mirror of Twilight in the light world because it was their design that the two worlds eventually meet, a true divine

---

21   See *The Legend of Zelda,; Ocarina of Time* 1998

boon. Her bitterness towards the light realm is overcome by the sheer power of Link and Zelda's virtuous deeds. What we have here is a clear glimpse of the profound Christian truth that, by the grace of God, the best of ends can be brought out of the worst of beginnings. If goodness and grace are given a chance, they can break the cycle of evil and create new beginnings. Though sin and evil result in fracture and disharmony, nevertheless, two estranged parties may yet reconcile and bitterness may yet be melted away into peace. An evil past does not fatalistically entail an unredeemed future and the faintest glimmers of hope can be fanned into the fullest flames of redemption.

Conclusion

The landscapes of *Twilight Princess* and Christian theology are rolling and varied, filled with themes that are as ancient as they are familiar. It would be hard to find a story or a worldview that does not include a story of origins, an explanation for why things are not the way they should be, an account of the various relationships within the world and a certain understanding of evil and redemption. The ubiquity of such distinct inklings and yearnings in human consciousness, as reflected in fictional narratives such as *Twilight Princess*, suggests that perhaps the collective imagination of humanity is onto something. The Christian Scriptures tell us that God providentially ordered the world such that people "would seek him and perhaps reach out for him and find him, though he is not far from any one of us."[22] In *Twilight Princess*, we have an example of such grasping, as the virtual landscape of *Twilight Princess* is painted with broad strokes of implicitly Christian themes. Landscapes of such beauty are worth gazing upon for an eternity.

---

22   Acts 17:27

Trouble in the Golden Realm: Ganondorf and Hyrule's Problem of Evil in Ocarina of Time

Jonathan L. Walls

As a particularly famous literary character once said, "Better to reign in Hell than serve in heaven."[1] Thus Satan contemplates his new lot in life, having been cast out of Heaven in John Milton's epic poem *Paradise Lost*. This amazing tale is an adaptation of the Bible's creation story found in the book of Genesis, in which Adam and Eve are tempted into the first sin by the serpent, Satan.[2] In the book of Genesis, as well as *Paradise Lost*, we witness the advent of this utterly wicked thing known as Sin.

The concept of some universal notion of evil lends itself perfectly to the art of storytelling. From the Garden of Eden to the command room of the Death Star, there is almost always some representation of basic goodness pitted against corrupt evil within popular myth. Whether it's Beowulf-Grendel, Frodo-Sauron, Cloud-Sephiroth, Notre Dame-Miami,[3] or Jesus-Satan, the tale of good versus evil is one that has resonated with humanity as long as human beings have been telling stories. Ganondorf, *The Legend of Zelda's* timeless antagonist, accurately represents universal evil, not only mirroring the corruption that can occur in human hearts on account of such evil, but causing similar consequences within the larger framework of *Zelda's* fiction.

It's not hard to see why the good vs. evil premise captivates us so much. On one hand, it evokes a basic human desire to see integrity

---

1   John Milton, *Paradise Lost* Book 1 Line 263.

2   The belief that this serpent either is or represents Satan is almost unanimous in orthodox Christian belief, although it is an inference based on a number of other texts and never explicitly stated.

3   See the Notre Dame-Miami, "Catholics vs. Convicts" football rivalry of the late 80's and early 90's

win out over injustice. No one likes to feel like he is on the raw end of an injustice in real life, so when we see these types of wrongs challenged head on and defeated in fiction, it naturally produces a feeling of deep satisfaction.

Every great drama needs some opposing force, a wrong or evil that must be put right. Shigeru Miyamoto and the creators of *Zelda* understand this, and so Ganondorf plays an indispensable role.

Although introduced in 1986 as the great *Zelda* antagonist in the revolutionary original *Legend of Zelda*, we see the beginning of Ganondorf's reign of terror, from a chronological standpoint, in the 1998 Nintendo 64 hit, *The Legend of Zelda; The Ocarina of Time*. Ganondorf, born to a race of thieves known as the Gerudo, is, in keeping with the mysterious nature of their race, the only male born into their numbers in a century. Born the Prince of Thieves, Ganondorf rises from trusted advisor to the throne of Hyrule, the majestic land where *Zelda* stories typically take place. Scheming behind the back of the king, Ganondorf plans to get his hands on the hallowed Triforce, the transcendent symbol of power, courage and wisdom in the land of Hyrule. Ganondorf understands the legends, which state that he who holds all three pieces of the Triforce, which is historically linked with the royal family of Hyrule, will be granted the desires of his heart. Desiring power above all else, Ganondorf plans to use his trusted position to get his hands on the sacred relic.

It doesn't take long to see the effects of Ganondorf's evil schemes. Even within the first section of the game, despite the brave young Link's best attempts to counter it, Ganondorf's wicked curse causes the death of the great Deku Tree, the ancient guardian of the elf-like Kokiri people.

Making Sense of Sin and Sins

Unfortunately for the Deku tree and a great many other victims of Ganondorf's evil curse, wickedness has similar effects in the Zelda universe as sin does in our world. As the apostle Paul writes: "For the wages of sin is death."[4] This is a point that the Christian faith makes very clear: *To sin is to separate oneself from God. To separate oneself from God is to die.* This truth is based on the fundamental Christian belief that God is perfect love,[5] and therefore cannot and will not tolerate sin, precisely because He loves us and hates anything that harms us or our true well being. John Wesley illuminates this idea in his sermon, *The Orignial, Nature, Property, and Use of the Law.* The "Law" is an ingrained notion of right and wrong that comes from God. "It pleased the great Creator to make these, his first-born sons, intelligent beings, that they might know him that created them. For this end he endued them with understanding, to discern truth from falsehood, good from evil…"[6]

Here, Wesley is speaking of God's impartation of the ability to discern between right and wrong to the angels. Satan, known then as Lucifer, is included. Wesley later discusses how this crucial discernment is passed onto mankind:

> …when He had raised man from the dust of the earth, breathed into him his breath of life, and caused him to become a living soul, endued with power to choose good or evil; he gave to this free, intelligent creature the same law as to his first-born children, -- not wrote, indeed, upon tables of stone, or any corruptible substance, but engraven on his heart by the finger of God…[7]

So, privy to such moral knowledge, it is humanity's choice to choose the "false" over the truth, or the "evil" over the good that defines sin.

---

4 Romans 6:23 NIV

5 This is a crucial and non-negotiable belief in the realm of Christianity. All reasonable theology must adhere to this point.

6 John Wesley Sermon, *Original, Nature, Property, and Use of The Law.* Wesley's sermons are available online.

7 Ibid.

Things get trickier when one attempts to begin identifying specific sins. Consider Ingo, the surly employee of Lon Lon Ranch in central Hyrule. Although his egregious mustache may automatically tip poor Ingo as a villain, he is actually a bit of an ambiguous character. He gripes and grouses about his workload under his employer Talon and then runs a barely-fair gambling racket out of the ranch when the newly empowered Ganondorf fires Talon.

We never see Ingo commit any outright atrocities like Ganondorf does. He sticks strictly to the letter of the law and to his word, even if it means backhandedly attempting to lock Link into the ranch after losing the prized horse Epona on a wager. (Hint: Simply use Epona to jump the fence.) We can't put our finger on any specific sins for Ingo, so he must be living the way he ought to, right?

Many bristle at the suggestion that something they do or believe may be considered sinful. While there are a number of specific sinful acts that are clearly pointed out and warned against in the Bible, the concept of sin cannot be reduced to a number of do's and don'ts. C.S. Lewis talks about the deeper issue of the nature of sin in *Mere Christianity*, a collection of essays based on a series of radio show appearances he made. In a talk called *The Great Sin*, Lewis details what he believes to be the most heinous and dangerous of all sins. About this sin, Lewis writes:

> There is no fault which makes a man more unpopular, and no fault which we are more unconscious of in ourselves. And the more we have it in ourselves, the more we dislike it in others. The Vice I am talking of is Pride or Self-Conceit; and the virtue opposite to it, in Christian morals, is called humility.[8]

---

8   C.S. Lewis, *Mere Christianity* (HarperSanFrancisco, 2001), 121.

Lewis further elaborates on this observation, "…it was through Pride that the devil became the devil[9]: ==Pride leads to every other vice: it is the complete anti-God state of mind.=="[10]

The notion of Pride as the central sin presented here by Lewis is a somewhat advanced and very important one for understanding Christian theology. The simplistic understanding and even caricature of sin among Christians and non-Christians alike has cast a shadow of misrepresentation over what Christ stood for, and indeed, still stands for among humans, not least of all in our modern culture.

A common criticism leveled at Christianity by non-believers is that Christians try incessantly to tie people to a set of rules to follow, designed to suck any fun out of life. The Christian God comes off looking like George Orwell's *Big Brother*.[11] But remember what Wesley said: the law which helps us know good, as well as sin, was "not wrote, indeed, upon tables of stone, or any corruptible substance, but engraven on his heart by the finger of God."

Pride, the central sin, as Lewis pointed out, is the "complete anti-God state of mind." This suggests that when a critic or proponent of Christianity attempts to reduce Christianity to a specific set of laws, he is misinformed on the topic, delivering an incomplete and inaccurate account of what Christianity's God of love stands for. While individual corrupt acts can and will spring out of sin, it must be understood that sin itself is like an infection, and individual sins are its symptoms. It taints not only the sinner, but those sinned against, and can even spread further. Our entire fallen world is mired in sin and consequently, even good things and great beauty are subject to death and destruction. ==This world is truly in need of a savior.==

---

9 A reference to the Christian belief that the devil, Lucifer, once a great angel, was cast out of the heavenly ranks for thinking himself great enough to challenge the throne of God.

10 *Mere Christianity*, 122.

11 See the novel *1984*

Ganondorf's Power-Play

In Lewis's articulation of Pride, the great Sin, he goes into more detail about what the manifestation of Pride and the sinful acts that follow can look like. These acts consist of all the evil and selfish acts that characterize the human condition. Let's take a look at what Lewis says about Pride and the lust for power.

> Now what you want to get clear is that sin is *essentially* competitive-it is competitive by its very nature--while the other vices are competitive, so to speak, by accident. Pride gets no pleasure out of having something, only out of having more of it than the next man...Of course, power is what Pride really enjoys: there is nothing makes a man feel so superior to others as being able to move them about like toy soldiers.[12]

Can't you just imagine Ingo, lying in bed at night, twisting his mustache, cursing Talon under his breath and believing himself more capable of ruling over the ranch? We even see him basking in his own self-conceit once he has been promoted to his higher position of ranch caretaker, delighting in his good standing with Ganondorf, his avenue to even more power. He emphatically tells Link:

> There are some people in Kakariko (Village) spreading rumors that I cheated Talon out of the ranch, but don't be ridiculous! That guy Talon was weak! I, the hard working Ingo, poured so much energy into this place! Listen, the great Ganondorf recognized my obvious talents and gave the ranch to me! I will raise a fine horse and win recognition from the great Ganondorf![13]

---

12   *Mere Christianity*, 122-123.
13   *The Legend of Zelda; Ocarina of Time*

Trouble in the Golden Realm

Along with being far too liberal with his use of the exclamation point, Ingo perfectly embodies what Lewis warns us about concerning the desire for power as a symptom of Pride. In the case of Ingo, his Pride has led him to a completely corrupt lifestyle, though he may not have broken a single law while getting there.

Ganondorf's influence doesn't stop with Ingo and Lon Lon Ranch. Ganondorf's own lust for power brings about widespread evil, just like the true nature of sin as Christians understand it.

As mentioned previously, we see the Death of the Great Deku tree. Like the curse of death that followed sin into our world, the curse of death is upon the ancient and benevolent tree in Zelda's world. Failing to obtain a sacred stone of the Forest that will play an integral role in his conquest for the Triforce, Ganondorf vengefully curses the tree, leaving it decimated, beyond hope of repair. Despite Link's heroics, in which he enters the life-giving tree itself and eradicates the evil within, the curse cannot be broken and Link must watch as the guardian of the Kokiri people withers away.

The tree tells Link and his fairy, "Because of that (Ganondorf's) curse, my end is nigh. Though your valiant attempts to break the curse were successful, I was doomed before you started."[14]

In Lewis' exposition of Pride, he brings his descriptions to an even more pragmatic, if wide-sweeping, conclusion. "Pride…goes on and on…it is pride which has been the chief cause of misery in every nation and every family since the world began."[15]

Consider what happens to Hyrule as the story of *Ocarina of Time* continues. As Link continues his quest, he has the opportunity to meet with Princess Zelda herself, as she had foreseen in her dreams. In this meeting, Link learns of Ganondorf's impending betrayal of Zelda's father, the King, and of his desire to obtain the Triforce. It is a plot that Zelda can sense, but cannot prove. Zelda's plan eventually sees Link

---

14   *The Legend of Zelda; Ocarina of Time*
15   *Mere Christianity*, 123-124.

enter the sacred Temple of Time in an attempt to safely seal away the Triforce. In a clever twist, the plan backfires and, as a result, Ganondorf obtains temporary control of Hyrule and Link is sealed away in a deep sleep.

Seven years later, Link awakens, ready at last to face his destiny and put right the evil curse that Ganondorf has brought upon Hyrule. When Link emerges, more destruction awaits him. Hyrule Castle Town, once a place of music, commerce and bustling activity, is now a desolate wasteland inhabited only by the undead. Zora's domain, once a sparkling haven of flowing water and abundant life, is now frozen over. Link's childhood home, Kokiri forest, is now overrun with monsters.

Ganondorf's actions are based on the way of life he has chosen and, like sin, cannot be reduced to a specific series of deeds. His selfish pursuit of power infects the world around him. Ganondorf diminishes Hyrule into a place devoid of joy. But joy is a concept quite beyond Ganondorf now. Remember, Lewis says, "Pride gets no pleasure out of having something, only out of having more of it than the next man."[16] Unfortunately for The Prince of Thieves, he can never have more power than *everyone*. Eventually, just like any human in pursuit of power, he will come up against the true source of power and will find himself not only lacking, but wretched and alone to boot. The quest for power, like any pursuit of sin, ends only in misery.

The point Lewis makes is that while there are certainly right and wrong ways to live and good and evil things that can be done, the way we ought to live is based on a crucial truth more basic than any individual rule, at least according to the teachings of Christianity. As Lewis states it: "In God you come up against something which is in every respect immeasurably superior to yourself. Unless you know God as that--and, therefore, know yourself as nothing in comparison--you do not know God at all."[17] The Christian life begins with submission to the will of God, which is perfect love. The rest will follow.

---

16   Ibid., 122.
17   Ibid., 124.

The Problem of Evil: Bigger Than Ganondorf

This leads us to the most fundamental problem, which, at first glance, seems as insurmountable as the race against the Greek-inspired Running Man in Hyrule.[18] Consider this ancient quote that is widely attributed to another famous Grecian:

> Is God willing to prevent evil, but not able? Then he is not omnipotent. Is he able, but not willing? Then he is malevolent. Is he both able and willing? Then whence cometh evil? Is he neither able nor willing? Then why call him God?

This statement, often credited to the Greek philosopher Epicurus, is more recently echoed and elaborated by 18th Century Scottish philosopher David Hume,[19] concisely summing up what is commonly known as The Problem of Evil. It seems a simple enough conclusion: If God is all-powerful and good, shouldn't He just snap his fingers and wipe out all crime, hate and injustice from the world? Better yet, why doesn't He go back to the beginning of time and prevent Evil from ever coming about in the first place?[20] (Does God have a magical time-turning ocarina?) This, perhaps above all others, is the issue that drives most people away from belief in God and creates the most

---

18   The Running Man can be found around Hyrule Field and is literally impossible to beat in a race.

19   David Hume, *Dialogues Concerning Natural Religion and the Posthumous Essays*, ed. Richard H. Popkin (Indianapolis: Hackett Publishing Company, 1980). See especially Parts X-XI.

20   At the end of Ocarina of Time, according to game director Eiji Aonuma, time is split into two separate universes. In one of them, Link and Zelda do this very thing, using their new knowledge to stop Ganondorf before he ever begins his campaign of terror: http://www.thehylia.com/index.php?subaction=showfull&id=1173582355&archive=

cognitive dissonance and gnawing uncertainty among believers.

Let's look at it in terms of the *Zelda* universe. Why don't the three goddesses Din, Farore and Nayru just destroy Ganondorf? Or why did they create a Hyrule in which an evil presence like Ganondorf can exist in the first place? Since we know, according to the mythology, that the three goddesses of Hyrule *do* at least exist, we are tempted to conclude that they either have not the power or the will to stop the evil. Or perhaps they just never foresaw the possibility for someone like Ganondorf, a suggestion that would be no small slight on their power in and of itself.

Now it may be fun to speculate possible answers to these questions, but the truth is most likely rolling around somewhere in Shigeru Miyamoto's brain and is not too terribly important anyway, because if Hyrule's problem of evil were solved in any of these ways, there wouldn't be much of a plot to build a game around.

But what do we say about the real God? The problem of evil suggests that either God does not exist, or He is not the God that Christianity makes Him out to be. The tangible fallout is that those who do not believe in God believe, rather, in what they can see all around them: a world that is as much good as bad, ugly as well as beautiful and seemingly indifferent to which is which. The conclusion is that the true mover and shaker in the universe is nothing more than nature and the results have followed a path like dominoes, helpless to stand and determined to fall.

Fortunately, like most issues worth thinking about, the character of God cannot be summed up and shut down wholesale by a simple logical problem that is, quite frankly, mired in human limitations and incomplete. We, as humans, sometimes think, quite rationally, that we would love the power to single-handedly wipe out all the evil in the world, but how would we do it, if we somehow possessed this magnificent power? Would we kill all the evildoers? Perhaps we could brainwash them into being good and selfless from now on. If we somehow got rid of them, wouldn't more pop up in their place? If Link kills Ganondorf, won't another power-hungry villain come along? If he banishes Ganondorf to the twilight realm, won't he eventually return?

That hypothetical scenario is dumbed down for sure, but it accurately represents the obstacle (yes, obstacle) that God Himself will not and, therefore, cannot overcome in order to achieve those ends: our own free will. This is what theologians refer to as God *self-limiting* His own power. But why would He do this? He could have easily manipulated every thought, action and instance in all of history to ensure that sin never came about.

To put it in an oversimplified,[21] logical statement, like the Greek proclamation on the problem of evil, we will say that God is perfect love and desires for us to *perfectly* love Him back. He won't settle for anything less than the best. The very definition of perfect love (as defined by God's very nature) is love that is *freely given*. Therefore, we *must* be free in order to love Him back the best way possible. If we are *truly* free, then the possibility to break from God's will--sin--*must* exist. Consequently, the only thing that can hinder God's plan for each of us is our free choice not to follow Him.[22]

So while it seems counterintuitive at first to imagine the omnipotent God limiting His own power, it turns out to be the best and wisest thing for God to do. John Wesley explains the issue:

> Were human liberty taken away men would be as incapable of virtue as stones. Therefore (with reverence be it spoken) the Almighty himself cannot do this thing.

---

21 There always can be, and are, further nuances and theories for such statements which, each in their own right, can (and do) fill countless books.

22 Nothing can derail God's ultimate plan, but we can choose to reject Him for ourselves. See C.S. Lewis's *The Great Divorce* for a fictional narrative based on this belief. Lewis also writes extensively on this subject in *The Problem of Pain*. For an excellent distillation of Lewis' arguments on the subject, check out Michael L. Peterson's essay "C.S. Lewis on the Necessity of Gratuitous Evil" in David Baggett, Gary R. Habermas and Jerry Walls, eds., *C.S Lewis as Philosopher; Truth, Goodness and Beauty* (Downers Grove: InterVarsity Press, 2008).

> He cannot thus contradict himself, or undo what he has done. He cannot destroy out of the soul of man that image of himself wherein he made him. And without doing this he cannot abolish sin and pain out of the world. But were it to be done it would imply no wisdom at all, but barely a stroke of omnipotence. Whereas all the manifold wisdom of God (as well as his power and goodness) is displayed in governing man as man; not as a stock or a stone, but as an intelligent and free spirit, capable of choosing either good or evil.[23]

It should be noted that this particular area of Christian doctrine is and has been one of the more hotly debated issues among Christians for hundreds of years. Beliefs on this topic range everywhere from the view that we are free in the "libertarian" sense that our choices are truly up to us and could have been done otherwise, to the belief that we are "free" only in the sense that we willingly "choose" to do whatever God has determined us to do. On the latter view, God in His sovereignty has unconditionally chosen for some persons to be saved and others to be eternally damned.[24] It's clear where Wesley stood on the latter.

For now, let's continue with the view that human beings are free in the sense that they are not determined and that their choices are truly up to them, since God has conferred such freedom on them. When an understanding of free will enters the picture, it takes us a long way toward understanding the existence of evil in the world. As we have pointed out, God cannot simply reach to earth and eradicate or stop all evil in its tracks in one fell swoop without compromising our free will,

---

23 John Wesley Sermon, *On Divine Providence*

24 For further details, see Jerry L. Walls and Joseph R. Dongell, *Why I am not a Calvinist* (Downers Grove: Intervarsity Press, 2004). See especially chapters 3-4.

an integral part of what gives us the ability to love God and others fully. At least, when God does finally do that, the jig will be up.[25]

Natural Evil, Naturally

But the issue is not completely resolved yet. There is still a Giant's Wallet full of suffering that the human race must endure that does not appear to be the result of free, evil actions. This is commonly known as *Natural Evil* and can include anything from cancer to an earthquake and many things in between. The problem is that all of this still happens on God's watch and is part of His creation.

This issue is mirrored in *The Ocarina of Time* as well. Take, for example, the beautiful Zora's Domain. What was once a place of sparkling water, flowing rivers and the best diving game in all of Hyrule becomes frozen over. Lake Hylia, another beautiful showcase of the goddess's creation, is drying up. It only takes one glance up at Death Mountain to see that things aren't right up there. (Especially for the poor saps who go up without the Hylian Shield.) Death befalls the very land of Hyrule.

To once again state things simply, Christians believe that when humanity fell into sin, they brought the natural world down with them. In other words, we are intimately related to the larger world of creation and our actions affect it, as well as ourselves. The story of the Garden of Eden from Genesis explains this and, whether one believes that to be literal or symbolic, the gist is the same. Sin entered the world and we are left with a world in need of saving. Like Hyrule, it retains large vestiges of its intended beauty, but death and imperfection are now part of the picture.

From a narrative standpoint, it is easy to see a purpose in all of these wicked things. Any good story contains a character arc, by which we see a hero or group of protagonists change by the end of the story.

---

25   Philippians 2:9-11

We see protagonists go from weak to strong, cowardly to courageous, embittered to loving, or any variation of these. The list of films, books and video games containing these story arcs is quite literally endless. We need these trials and setbacks to craft a compelling tale. We need Link to drag his lazy butt out of bed and realize his own strength. We need him to be beset by Ganondorf's evil plans. We need him to pass, quite literally, through Fire and Shadow[26] and come out all the stronger.

As great art is known to do, these repeated themes just might be able to show us something about the truth of life. In *Evil and the God of Love,* John Hick discusses the purposes and merits of human suffering. He says, "The contribution which Sin and its attendant suffering make to God's plan does not exist in any value intrinsic to themselves but, on the contrary, in the activities whereby they are overcome, namely redemption from sin, and men's mutual service amid suffering."[27]

The suggestion here is that the anguish which pervades our world serves a greater purpose by refining us into the people that God intends us to be. This is a lifelong process, but we constantly see small-scale examples of it. A rough patch in life may leave us stronger and capable of loving even more deeply. A mistake leaves us wiser, if we allow ourselves to learn.

But what of *gratuitous* natural evils, which have no discernible greater purpose whatsoever? Perhaps we cannot attribute such gratuitous evils to the free-will argument, or the belief that God will bring about something better, or possibly prevent a worse evil in this life, through the tragedy. These horrendous disasters happen all the time. So what do we make of gratuitous natural evil?

Some argue that we, as humans, simply cannot know whether or not God will bring about something greater through the tragedy,

---

26 Two of the Temples Link must traverse on his journey- The Fire Temple and The Shadow Temple

27 John Hick, *Evil and the God of Love* (New York: Harper & Row, 1978), 323.

that our scope is far too limited to makes such claims. However, C.S. Lewis sees no issue with unbridled natural evil, which he discusses in *The Problem of Pain*. According to Lewis, a natural order, which is *not* necessarily directly controlled by the hand of God at all times, is actually essential to accommodate truly free beings. Lewis says: "A creature with no environment would have no choices to make: so that freedom, like self-consciousness (if they are not indeed the same thing) again demands the presence to the self of something other than the self."[28] Michael L. Peterson elaborates on Lewis' position in the following:

> But a natural order also entails the possibility of natural evil. God cannot simply arrange all natural evils so that they never harm us out of proportion to some higher good at which he aims, since so doing would involve frequent interruption or alteration of the world and thereby jeopardize the very meaning of a natural system. Lewis' conclusion, then, is not that gratuitous natural evils are necessary…but that *it is necessary that gratuitous natural evil be possible.*[29]

So, it seems that, much like the *possibility* of human sin and bad choices based on free will, the *possibility* of natural evil must exist in our fallen world.

The Hero of Time

Consider these words from Hick on Christ's death: "For the sake of mankind Christ fulfilled the pattern of redemptive suffering. For the Church has always believed as one of its cardinal doctrines that the judicial murder of the Christ was the focus of God's redemptive work

---

28   C.S. Lewis, *The Problem of Pain* (New York: Macmillan, 1962), 29.
29   *C.S. Lewis as Philosopher*, 189

and the turning point of man's salvation."[30]

The death and resurrection of Christ was not only the apex of God's ultimate story arc and the very picture of our victory over death through Jesus, but it is a large-scale representation of how our own suffering can lead to small gains and victories, even within the framework of our lives on earth. The ultimate truth in the matter is that whatever agony, trial or misery may beset us, be it the cause of free will or natural evil, we have complete assurance that, through Christ, we will have victory. This means ultimately and completely beating the curse of death and living forever with God. The apostle Paul practically trash talks death, "Where, Oh death, is your victory? Where, oh death, is your sting? The sting of death is in sin, and the power of sin is in the law. But thanks be to God! He gives us the victory through our Lord Jesus Christ."[31]

In your darkest hour, whether it's a frustrating run through the dreaded Water Temple, or a period when you are tempted to despair in your real life, rest assured that nothing happens outside of God's control and even the fiercest betrayals of His love can be used for His glory and serve His ultimate good purposes.[32]

---

30 *Evil and the God of Love*, 355-356
31 1 Cornithians 15: 55-57 NIV
32 See Romans 8:38-39

The Birth of Gaming from the Spirit of Fantasy: Video Games as Secondary Worlds with Special Reference to The Legend of Zelda and J. R. R. Tolkien [§0]

Philip Tallon [§70]

[To begin go to §1.]

§0 ABSTRACT: This entire essay could be seen as a footnote to Tolkien's "On Fairy Stories," an addendum that explores the possibility of video games as a medium for *Faërie*, with special reference to *The Legend of Zelda*, the fantasy game *ne plus ultra*. The ultimate intention of this essay is to offer, by connection with Tolkien's profound and theologically informed thoughts on fairy stories, a more redeeming paradigm for video games than sheer entertainment. Seeing video games through this lens pays them the burdensome compliment of suggesting that they might reflect some gleams of divine light.

§1 The story has been told and retold, until it has taken on legendary status, of Shigeru Miyamoto lighting a lantern and going down into that cave:

> One day, when he was seven or eight, he came across a hole in the ground. He peered inside and saw nothing but darkness. He came back the next day with a lantern and shimmied through the hole and found himself in a small cavern. He could see that passageways led to other chambers. Over the summer, he kept returning to the cave to marvel at the dance of the shadows on the walls.[1]

---

1   "Master of Play: The Many Worlds of a Video-Game Artist." *New Yorker*, December 20 and 27, 2010, 86.

This bit of childhood biography, like all stories from childhood, is better taken as a suggestive symbol than a causal determinant for the character of Miyamoto's later work. But it *is* suggestive. And Miyamoto has told the story many times, no doubt, because it captures some essential nutrient in his creations: *the wonder of exploration, the discovery of new worlds*. Childish wonder animates Miyamoto's most famous creations. The *Mario* and *Zelda* series are marked by a pervading sense of joyful discovery: from the way that coins and other goodies appear from special blocks that Mario hits with his head, to Link's ability to explore a vast world with hundreds of hidden secrets (even in the first 8-bit *Zelda*).

(There is, also, a more literal element of "exploring hidden caves" in Miyamoto's work, like the way that, in *Zelda*, Link discovers hidden caves and explores them.)

Discovery is an essential part, if not THE essence, of childhood and Miyamoto's games offer an opportunity to explore and discover within the fenced worlds he creates. *Zelda's* world, Hyrule, is, in Miyamoto's words, "a miniature garden that you can put into a drawer and revisit any time you like." (NY, 92)

[For an introduction to *The Legend of Zelda*, go to §2. To begin reading about J. R. R. Tolkien's "On Fairy Stories," go to §3]

§2 You open the package for *The Legend of Zelda*. Unlike the plastic gray of the rest of Nintendo's offerings, this cartridge is shiny and golden. This is the first gold cartridge you've ever seen. It's unknown to you at this time, but this cartridge is also the first NES game to have a battery in it, so that it saves your progress. This is important because this game is long. Unlike *Super Mario Bros.*, you cannot beat it in a single sitting. Also unknown to you until a few weeks later is, if you take the game out without turning off the NES's power, it wipes all the memory, which is what you do to your friend's *Legend of Zelda* game at a sleepover.

You pop the gold cartridge into your NES. After choosing your name, the first screen you see is a large field of light brown, edged by boulders that look like they have been dyed green for St. Patrick's day. The music sets in instantly, a sprightly chiptune that is difficult to describe, except that it is reminiscent of pageantry. You could march soldiers to it. But the gallant, old-world music is also mixed in with a more somber theme. Minor chords suggest that all is not well in the land of wherever-you-are.

You are an elvish pipsqueak about three steps further along the evolutionary ladder than Pac-Man. If Pac-Man was Ludo Africanus, you at least are Ludo Habilis.

Immediately ahead of you is a black square which you enter and meet a bearded wizard standing between two 8-bit fires. He tells you, "It's dangerous to go alone! Take this." You step forward and pick up a wooden sword. A satisfying musical sting plays as your avatar holds the sword aloft.

You leave the cave and now face a choice. You can go north, east or west in this game. This is new. Previously, you had only played games like *Super Mario Bros*. These were side-scrollers, platform games that forced you to move in one overall direction. But here you have a choice. You go north and the screen shifts to another verdantly rocky landscape, this time with moving objects. Crawling around the screen are gourd-shaped creatures without legs. These, you find out later, are called Octoroks and they shoot rocks at you out of the fluted ends of their mouths, presumably propelled by pneumatic pressure. Their resemblance to octopuses is made more obvious in later versions of the game.

Your shield deflects the rocks. Your sword, when you stab out with it, fires a silvery version of itself across the screen. You "shoot" your sword at one of the Octoroks and kill it. You discover that stabbing makes you vulnerable. When you stab again, one of the projectile rocks catches you with your shield to the side. You emit a tiny, unpleasant digital "ppmm" sound, lose half a heart and now your sword no longer shoots.

After running around and killing a few more Octoroks, you get jewels, which you collect by merely absorbing them while walking through them. On killing the final Octorok, (the final one was an ADD fellow who seemed content merely to run all around the screen rather than pursue you) you pick up a heart. This brings your health up to full and you can shoot your sword again.

Again, you have to choose which direction to go. You can go east or west. You go west and encounter jumping four-legged spider creatures (Tektites), which are much more difficult to kill. You sustain some damage, but live to fight another day. Eventually, you travel east as well, fighting bulldogs (Moblins) who shoot arrows, and who provide more of a strategic challenge to kill. They shoot arrows much faster than the Octoroks spit rocks, so sliding your shield to the side to shoot your sword must be done more carefully.

You begin to wonder what to do with all the coins you collected. In a seaside area, you find a cave and buy bombs. Now you wonder what to do with them. They're clumsy weapons that leave the rocks unaffected. Later, fooling around with the bombs to kill Tektites, you blow open a hidden black square indicating a dungeon. You descend.

[For more *Zelda*, go to §7a; to read about J. R. R. Tolkien's "On Fairy Stories," go to §3]

§3 In March of 1939, J. R. R. Tolkien adventured from Oxford up to the University of Saint Andrews in Scotland to deliver the prestigious and horribly underfunded Andrew Lang lecture. His honorarium was only £30. His subject was fairy stories, which was fitting because Lang had been a world-renowned editor of fairy tale collections (most famously, *The Blue Fairy Book*).

Tolkien's lecture, eventually published as a mammoth 20,000+ word essay, did as much for fairy tales as Freud did for dreams. It legitimized (or perhaps restored) them as a subject worthy of serious scrutiny. In his essay, Tolkien clears away the Tinkerbell-image of fairy tales to get to their essence: not an impish creature but a place–*Faërie*– which is as substantial and significant (in Tolkien's mind) as any this-worldly locale. *Faërie's* citizens are not merely "fairies" or even "elves" (the proper connotation of the word), but also

> dwarfs, witches, trolls, giants, or dragons: it holds the seas, the sun, the moon, the sky; and the earth, and all things that are in it: tree and bird, water and stone, wine and bread, and ourselves, mortal men, when we are enchanted...Stories that are actually concerned primarily with "fairies," that is with creatures that might also in modern English be called "elves," are relatively rare, and as a rule not very interesting. Most good "fairy-stories" are about the adventures of men in the Perilous Realm or upon its shadowy marches...The definition of a fairy-story--what it is, or what it should be--does not, then, depend on any definition or historical account of elf or fairy, but upon the nature of Faërie: the Perilous Realm itself, and the air that blows in that country.[2]

Faërie is a kind of parallel world (a sideways universe), whose circle overlaps with our own from time to time. The circles of the magic and the mundane overlap to create a Venn diagram whose intersection, for those from our world, results in shades of enchantment.

Tolkien's essay is an exercise in cartography of this Perilous Realm, as he charts some of the key features of the "secondary world" of the fairy tale. For the rest of this essay, I will discuss four important landmarks of this secondary world and suggest that *The Legend of Zelda* might well occupy a corner of the kingdom.

§4 *Fantasy and Secondary Worlds.* Tolkien's concept of secondary worlds is, on the surface, fairly straightforward. It's a fictional world

---

2   J. R. R. Tolkien, "On Fairy Stories" in *The Monsters and the Critics and Other Essays* (London: Harper Collins, 1997), 113-4.

that contrasts with the primary world. Through mimetic art, *homo faber*, man the maker, gives a kind of life to little worlds of his own. The act of making a secondary world is what Tolkien calls "subcreation." Tolkien's Christian theology clearly dictates that only God has the power to create *ex nihilo* (out of nothing). *Imaginative* human making is, then, in one sense, nothing more than the ability to pick up the deck of facts about the world and give it a shuffle. Tolkien writes, "The human mind, endowed with the powers of generalization and abstraction, sees not only *green-grass*, discriminating it from other things...but sees that it is *green* as well as being *grass*." This "invention of the adjective" is, for Tolkien, a bit of powerful magic, which could take the descriptor green from grass and apply it to the sun. Or could imaginatively alchemize the world (through the imagination) making gray metals golden, making heavy things light, giving men the bodies of horses, or mixing octopuses and cannons to create new creatures.[3] Using this power of fantasy, the power to shuffle the created realities of the world, "new form is made; Faërie begins; Man becomes a sub-creator."[4]

The epitome of fantastic subcreation is, for Tolkien, found in fairy tales. But this bit of linguistic magic, Tolkien thought, did not translate well to media that were primarily visual. This opens up an initial challenge, then, to whether visual media such as paintings, plays or video games can fully *be* fairy tales.

[To slay this objection, go to §5. To skip it go to §6.]

§5 *Can a Video Game be a Fantasy?* For Tolkien, the fantastic subcreation finds its most natural home in the realm of language. "In human art Fantasy is a thing best left to words, to true literature. In painting, for instance, the visible presentation of the fantastic image is technically too easy; the hand tends to outrun the mind, even to

---

3   Ibid., 122.
4   Ibid.

overthrow it."[5] Drama, even worse, for Tolkien, "is naturally hostile to Fantasy. Fantasy, even of the simplest kind, hardly ever succeeds in Drama...Men dressed up as talking animals may achieve buffoonery or mimicry, but they do not achieve Fantasy."[6]

A central objection Tolkien raises is that by visualizing the "magic," one short-circuits fantasy's power to interact with the deepest resources of the human mind's imagination. The argument here would seem to be that because fantasy depends primarily on an *imaginative* interaction with the land of *Faërie*, to trick one's eye into seeing *Faërie* cuts the imaginative capacity out of the loop, or perhaps overwhelms it.

> Drama has, of its very nature, already attempted a kind of bogus, or shall I say substitute, magic: *the visible and audible presentation of imaginary men in a story.* That is, in itself, an attempt to counterfeit the magician's wand. To introduce, even with mechanical success into this quasi-magical secondary, a further fantasy or magic is to demand, as it were, an inner or tertiary world. It is a world too much. To make such a thing may not be impossible. I have never seen it done with success.[7]

Tolkien's argument here seems to be that the flavor of special effects or clever costuming covers up the unique and delicate taste of enchantment. Visual representation and literary imagination are, for Tolkien, a bad wine-food pairing.

However, we should note that "I have never seen it done" is not the same as "it cannot be done." Tolkien's argument here is basically an inductive one. It moves from particular observations to universal conclusions, as in the following argument: All observed swans are white, therefore all swans are probably white. The universal conclusions of

---

5 Ibid., 140.
6 Ibid.
7 Ibid., 141.

any inductive argument can always be punctured by observing literal or metaphorical "black swans."

Therefore, we may simply say that *The Legend of Zelda* is one of the black swans and leave it at that. Many, many players experience in the land of Hyrule not merely excitement, but enchantment.

One gamer, speaking on the *Stupidnerd* game podcast, described his imaginative experience with the first *Legend of Zelda*. Entranced by not only the gameplay, but also the world, the gamer, on receiving from Nintendo Power a map of Hyrule with blank spaces at the edges, fills in the blank spaces with additional screens of his own creation. Another described the way that, after filling in a vaginal and scatological name for the main character (in *Zelda*, you can rename Link whatever you want), the player soon felt bad and changed the name back to Link. The intrusion of eighth-grade humor broke the spell, and so the joke had to go.[8]

However, there is an additional counter to Tolkien's argument. It may well be that Tolkien's criticism of stagecraft simply doesn't apply to Miyamoto's creations. The *Lord of the Rings* author accuses visual representation as being a kind of counterfeit magic, but mainly on the ground that they aim to trick the eye into seeing what ought to exist properly in the imagination. While words themselves are visual (or aural) representations, they provide us with the opportunity to "see through" them to the wider story. What if literal seeing could likewise provide a chance to "see through" the image to a land beyond?

The 8-bit world of Hyrule could hardly be said to trick the eye. The images on the screen are nearly as abstract as words themselves. The programmer's hand does not "overrun the mind" in the early versions of the game, to be sure. But it is noteworthy that, as the series has progressed and the graphics have become more sophisticated, Hyrule has retained a level of abstraction. It is as if Miyamoto is aware of

---

8 Stupidnerd Podcast, "#27 The Legend of Zelda" http://www.mysterycove.libsyn.com/stupid-nerd-27-legend-of-zelda (accessed June 20, 2011).

Tolkien's worry that visual tricks might cancel out the imagination, and so intentionally hangs onto the charming children's book quality of the first games. Because of this, "seeing" in *Zelda* always retains an element of "seeing as."

> [If you still agree with Tolkien, go to §x (End of Essay). If you agree with me, go to section §6.]

§6 Assuming then, that there is no barrier to video games being fairy tales because of the medium's visual form, let us proceed to discuss some of the deep connections between *The Legend of Zelda* and fairy tales.

> [Go to §7 to look at the connection between fantasy, secondary worlds and *Zelda*.]

> [Go to §8 to look at the way that *Zelda* can help us escape reality and recover a sense of wonder about the world.]

> [Go to §9 to look at the way that video games embody Tolkien's principle of consolation.]

§7 Recall, again, how Miyamoto describes Hyrule as a "miniature garden." This comment is accurate in that his worlds invite exploration even among the very young. But in size, there is nothing miniature about Hyrule. Even the first, 8-bit version of Hyrule is strikingly large. It was also open in a way that few other games had been previously. In fact, *The Legend of Zelda* was one of the first open world (or sandbox) games, a style of game that now proliferates. Playing it in 1988, without aid of a map or YouTube tutorials, finding one's way through the levels to the various dungeons was a herculean labor.

Adding to the difficulty were spacial puzzles built into the game. These were physical anomolies programmed into Hyrule. For example, to access certain areas, one had to go repeatedly up then left, again and again within a repeating screen until a secret area was unlocked. Yet the pleasures of the game far outweighed the frustrations.

§7a Having blown open the secret area, you feel a tingle of pleasure, not just at what you find inside (a giant heart piece, which increases the number of hearts in your health rating to four), but in the idea that secret areas like these fill the nooks and crannies of Hyrule. You frantically bomb other screens, finding nothing. Yet, you are still excited by the prospect of a game created by a designer who prodigally fills his world with buried treasures, something you have experienced only so far (in a much more limited way) playing *Super Mario Bros.* Unbeknownst to you at the time, this is another game authored by Miyamoto.

You wander around for long stretches at a time. This is an activity you find pleasant because of the simple attractiveness of the environment, even though Hyrule's landscapes look as if they were designed by Frank Lloyd Wright. The rock walls, shrubs and lakes could be used to test the accuracy of your compass's 90° angle, but they still suggest more of nature than anything else in the vicinity of your Florida suburb. This is a pleasant place. A good world.

Eventually you discover a screen with a withered tree that has a yawning dark mouth shaped like a doorway. You go through the door. You descend into the underworld. The screen changes; it goes dark.

§7b Tolkien's word for worlds of our own creation was "secondary world." When we enter into such a world we develop "secondary beliefs": understandings of the rules of the world. Samuel Taylor Coleridge spoke of the way that the imagination enters into a fictive world through the "willing suspension of disbelief." Yet Tolkien differs from how Coleridge construes our interaction with a fiction:

> What really happens is that the story-maker proves a successful "sub-creator." He makes a Secondary World which your mind can enter. Inside it, what he relates is "true": it accords with the

laws of that world. You therefore believe it, while you are, as it were, inside. The moment disbelief arises, the spell is broken; the magic, or rather art, has failed. You are then out in the Primary World again, looking at the little abortive Secondary World from outside.

Good secondary worlds, for Tolkien, display a rock-solid internal consistency built on fantastic premises. This "elvish craft," if accomplished, is "a rare achievement" but a valuable one for "story-making in its primary and most potent mode."

Tolkien clearly took his own advice, filling Middle-Earth with fantasy which displayed a tight internal logic, not only in the ordering of its metaphysics and history, but even down to the creation of grammars for his imaginary languages, including two Elvish languages (Quenya and Sindarin). When Tolkien did make changes to his secondary world that might introduce fictive "bugs" into his literary operating system, he patched them with meta-commentary.

One example is the notable change Tolkien made to the "Riddles in the Dark" chapter of *The Hobbit* between the first and second editions. In the first edition, Bilbo bests Gollum at the riddle contest and Gollum willingly cedes the contest and the ring. After beginning *The Lord of the Rings,* Tolkien realized that, the ring being what it is, Gollum would never give it up without a fight. So Tolkien changed the chapter, but incorporated the original version of the story into the world of Middle-Earth by suggesting that the first version of the story was a slight fib told by Bilbo about his possession of the ring. And those alternate versions of the text still existed because the keepers of Bilbo's legacy (Frodo, Sam, Merry and Pippen) could not believe that Bilbo would steal the ring, and so kept the original, innocent-er version of the story alive.

§7c *The Legend of Zelda* series shows nothing in its design to indicate a Tolkienian level of consistency and planning. Yet the fan community has puzzled over how the games relate to one another, spawning many theories. There does seem to be some effort on the game maker's part to create a certain level of continuity. (For instance, one game, *The Minish Cap*, explains the presence of rupees in the grass by appealing to tiny people called Picori.) The most consistent theory is that most of the stories featuring Link as the hero are their own "Legends" of *Zelda*: refracted accounts of a single urtext.

§7d Stepping beyond the worlds of Tolkien and Miyamoto, an additional connection between Tolkien's prescriptions and proscriptions about fantasy suggests itself. Games themselves are secondary, "fantastic" worlds, set apart from real life, yet also fundamentally embodying a tight, internal logic.

In *Homo Ludens*, a classic text about the element of play across human culture, Johan Huizinga describes the way that two main imperatives of play, play's freedom from real life and its seriousness, are bound together like twin stars. Play, for Huizinga, is "free" in that it is never compelled and takes place in a world apart from the domain of chores, taxes and oil changes. We don't have to do it. When we play, we step out of the real world into another world. Yet the play world has its own binding obligations. Huizinga's example is of a child sitting in the front row of four chairs, "playing 'trains,'" and warning his father not to "kiss the engine, Daddy, or the carriages won't think it's 'real.'"[9] Huizinga: "The inferiority of play is continually being offset by the corresponding superiority of its seriousness. Play turns to seriousness and seriousness to play."[10] This element of seriousness leads into the orderliness of play. "Play demands order absolute and supreme. The least deviation from it 'spoils the game,' robs it of its character and makes it worthless."[11] In *Man, Play, and Games*, Roger Callois affirms Huizinga's insights, noting that among the necessary attributes of play are play's being free (uncompelled), set apart from normal life and rule-bound.[12]

---

9   Johan Huizinga, *Homo Ludens: A Study of the Play Element in Culture* (Boston: Beacon, 1950), 8.

10   Ibid.

11   Ibid., 10.

12   Roger Caillois, "The Definition of Play, The Classification of Games"

Following Huizinga and Caillois, then, we can see that play is itself a kind of secondary world, apart from the restrictions of normal life but with its own unique laws of natural selection, gravitation and thermodynamics. What is important to keep in mind is how creation of the secondary world (ludic or fictive) depends on the underlying "rules." Written in a programming language more arcane than Elvish, glitches in video game play, stemming from bugs in the code or an incomplete system of rules and rewards, shatters the world of the game, annoying the players, perhaps causing them to quit.

A world done right, however, allows within itself an infinite variety of unpredicted possibilities that emerge from the law-like properties of the world. Within secondary worlds, humans can test their ingenuity, explore new possibilities, discover the limits of the game and the limits of their skills. Tom Bissell, writing about the unique experience which video games offer, highlights the explorative quality of games:

> The best part of looking up at a night sky, after all, is not any one star but the infinite possibility of what is between stars. Games often provide an approximation of this feeling, with the difference that you can find out what is out there. Teeming with secrets, hidden areas, and surprises that may pounce only on the second or third (or fourth) play-through...video games favor a form of storytelling that is, in many ways, completely unprecedented.[13]

§7e Returning to Tolkien, it is hard not to see the deep connections between a properly constructed game world and a properly constructed fantasy world.

Readers, having just finished *The Hobbit* and *Lord of the Rings*, often discover on library shelves or Tolkien's author page on Amazon.

---

in *The Game Design Reader*, eds. Katie Salen and Eric Zimmerman (Cambridge, Mass: MIT Press, 2006) 128.

13 Tom Bissell, *Extra Lives: Why Video Games Matter* (New York: Vintage, 2010), 13.

com "more" Middle-Earth in *The Silmarillion* or *Morgoth's Ring*. Getting the book home, the enthusiast first reads with pleasure, then bewilderment, and finally crushing boredom, the background mythology of Middle-Earth. Yet, after working up a bit of determination, the budding Tolkien scholar begins to discover in this mass of Elvish arcana a surplus of insight into the deeper workings of *Arda* (Middle-Earth).

To leap from Tolkien's popular works into his wider mythology sends one back into the story of the hobbits with increased appreciation and insight. Tolkien's work is akin to Miyamoto's "miniature garden." It is a "miniature cosmos" in which the avid reader can explore. Thus, not only can video games serve as a medium for fairy tales, but the canon of Tolkien's literary work provides a kind of game world within which we can play. Though it does not present itself explicitly, as such, the vast textual, thematic, mythological and metaphysical interconnections in the Middle-Earth canon allow for the kind of authored-but-open explorative experience found in many video games.

§8 *Escape and Recovery*. Two more necessary attributes of the fairy tale, for Tolkien, are derived from how the fantastic form plays tug-o'-war with reality. Escape allows us to pull away from reality and recovery pulls us back into it with renewed appreciation.

[To read about escape, read §8a-e, to skip to recovery, go to §8d]

§8a In *On Fairy Stories*, Tolkien defends the word "escape" from the negative moral judgment that has been attached to it:

> I have claimed that Escape is one of the main functions of fairy-stories, and since I do not disapprove of them, it is plain that I do not accept the tone of scorn or pity with which "Escape" is now so often used: a tone for which the uses of the word outside literary criticism give no warrant at all...Escape is evidently as a rule very practical, and may even be heroic..Evidently we are

faced by a misuse of words, and also by a confusion of thought. Why should a man be scorned if, finding himself in prison, he tries to get out and go home? Or if, when he cannot do so, he thinks and talks about other topics than jailers and prison-walls?[14]

For Tolkien, there is no harm at all in an attempt to "escape" from the ugliness and evil of modern life. Working at dehumanizing jobs, living in concrete cities, surrounded by injustice, Tolkien sees the human condition as less-than-optimal. Why should we blame those who do not want their art to be a mere reflection of the ugliness of the world? Tolkien: "Why should we not escape from or condemn the 'grim Assyrian' absurdity of top-hats, or the Morlockian horror of factories?"[15]

Tolkien rejects the idea that the world of *Faërie* (filled with beauty, goodness and truth) is less "real" than our modern world. Tolkien responds sharply to a clerk of Oxford he heard who welcomed the roar of traffic and the proximity of a factory because it brought students closer to "real life":

> The maddest castle that ever came out of a giant's bag in a wild Gaelic story is not only much less ugly than a robot-factory, it is also (to use a very modern phrase) "in a very real sense" a great deal more real.

Tolkien's Christianity grounds this conviction, finding an ever deeper, more redeeming purpose behind the "escape" into the beautiful world of *Faërie*. If ultimate reality is not ugly, unjust and depressing, but is, instead, beautiful, just and inspiring (as Christian theology holds), then the Christian does not believe that fairy tales lie to us about reality.

---

14   Tolkien, "On Fairy Stories," 148.
15   Ibid., 150.

Rather, in their tales of goodness, magic and wonder, they bring us into closer contact with the basic truth about the universe. In a famous poem "Mythopoeia," Tolkien offered this argument in verse:

> Yes! 'wish-fulfilment dreams' we spin to cheat
> our timid hearts and ugly Fact defeat!
> Whence came the wish, and whence the power to dream.[16]

If Christianity is true, the "wish-fulfillment dream" of fantasy is not a lie. On a deeper level, it is truer than the ugly "Facts" of the modern world. What's more, the very power of fantasy, Tolkien suggests, the power to dream, suggests that good wishes come from *beyond* the world of ugly facts, evil and death. Seen in this light, the escape of fantasy is a kind of escape *into* reality.

Yet, Tolkien does see that we might abuse fantasy. Perhaps by staying too long in *Faërie*, the "Escape of the Prisoner" might turn into the "Flight of the Deserter."[17] Here, perhaps more than anywhere else, the connections between Tolkien's essay and video gaming might strike a note of fear for the gamer. Though many hours of joyful escape often are opened up through video games like *Zelda*, any honest gamer knows the feeling of "desertion," abandoning duties for more play. No matter the age, desertions of duty, large and small, happen for the avid gamer: skipping class, dodging chores, neglecting family or even neglecting other pleasures (good food, outdoors, reading books)–all for the sake of "more." Honest gamers know this nearly invisible line that separates "escape" and "desertion." And they also know that on the far side of escape, the pleasures of play are often greatly diminished. "More play" does not always render "more pleasure."

§8b When you were ten, your parents divorced, pushing your mother into the job market and you and your sister into the status of latchkey children. You moved from a neighborhood in Oklahoma, with

---

16   J. R. R. Tolkien, "Mythopoeia" http://home.agh.edu.pl/~evermind/jrrtolkien/mythopoeia.htm (accessed June 20th, 2011).
17   Ibid., 148.

The Birth of Gaming from the Spirit of Fantasy

an undeveloped field behind your house where you played for hours, climbing trees and exploring, to a neighborhood in Florida where you were required to stay inside after school. Your hours between school and your mother's arrival home were large tracts of unconstructed time for reading and watching cartoon reruns. During these years, you first discovered *The Legend of Zelda,* a world into which you could escape, explore, save princesses, fight monsters and win.

§8c As you enter the dungeon buried beneath the hollow tree, you enter a dim, nicely-tiled room surrounded by open or locked doorways. The music changes from the wistful pomp of the over-world to a dark, repetitive tune (it sounds like *The Phantom of the Opera* riffing with one hand on a Casio keyboard).

Fighting your way through, you must figure out puzzles, as above. Again, the hidden secrets in the dungeon invite a curiosity and need to test and push the limits of the world. Eventually, you fight a fire-breathing dragon and receive as your reward a piece of the Triforce, an isosceles bit of magic reminiscent of the ring of power from Tolkien. Though this is unknown to you at the time, these are pieces of the Triforce of Wisdom, broken into eight parts to keep Ganon (Hyrule's Sauron) from gaining control of it. But this is irrelevant for your enjoyment because you already understand the concept of the MacGuffin, the letters of transit, the secret plans, the special-thing-everybody-wants, Boardwalk, Park Place, the king in checkmate.

As you pick up the glowing triangle, an orgasmic musical tune plays and you are deposited back at the mouth of the tree outside the dungeon. You are satisified. You plan to stop the game for a while and do your social studies homework, but you journey off in search of the next dungeon. "Just one more level," you tell yourself: a promise that you may break, forcing you to hurriedly and sloppily finish your homework later that night, before breakfast, or never."

MY LIFE!

§8d Shigeru Miyamoto, when asked for autographs by avid gamers, often signs his name and writes, "On sunny days, play outside."[18]

§8e Journeying out from the dungeon, you once again have to fight more enemies, though now they have a kind of pleasant familiarity. You like being in the over-world, wandering through the mountains or by the sea and fending off these species.

One thing you notice here is the way that the creatures are all similar to real world or mythological creatures you already know, with slight differences. There are: Crab-like Tektites that jump around like spiders; Armos, armor-clad with some ursine DNA mixed in there somewhere; Bulldog-faced Moblins; Cactile flying plants called Peahats.

In later games, this pattern of slight strangeness will continue. In Miyamoto's fantasy world, familiar animals are morphically a bit different and given different names: chickenish creatures are called Cuccoos, bat-like creatures are called Keese, etc. Hyrule's cocktail of strangeness and familiarity gives you an immense pleasure as it elevates those elements you recognize into the world of fantasy, while also making you feel welcome in this world.

§8f Escape, in Tolkien's sense, is already connected to recovery, in that escape from the world's ugliness and misery can be an escape into a deeper truth about the world. Eru Ilúvatar is in our world as well, known by a different name. But there's another connection. Fantasy helps us see the beauty of our own world more clearly, wiping off the dust of familiarity. Fantasy pulls us away from our world, but also pushes us back into it with renewed pleasure and awakened perception.

Tolkien:

But the true road of escape from such weariness is not to be

---

18   Nintendo Facts and Details, http://factsanddetails.com/japan.php?itemid=787&catid=21&subcatid=144 (accessed July 25th, 2011).

found in the wilfully awkward, clumsy, or misshapen, not in making all things dark or unremittingly violent; nor in the mixing of colours on through subtlety to drabness, and the fantastical complication of shapes to the point of silliness and on towards delirium. Before we reach such states we need recovery. We should look at green again, and be startled anew (but not blinded) by blue and yellow and red. We should meet the centaur and the dragon, and then perhaps suddenly behold, like the ancient shepherds, sheep, and dogs, and horses— and wolves. This recovery fairy-stories help us to make. In that sense only a taste for them may make us, or keep us, childish.... Recovery (which includes return and renewal of health) is a re-gaining—regaining of a clear view...We need, in any case, to clean our windows; so that the things seen clearly may be freed from the drab blur of triteness or familiarity.[19]

Breathing the air of Faërie for a while may help you see our own world afresh.

§8g All games, as Roger Caillois writes in *Man, Play and Games*, involve make believe. They are "accompanied by a special awareness of a second reality or of a free unreality, as against real life."[20] Games and fantasy both create worlds that are distinct from our own, but both highlight and make us increasingly aware of elements of this world. Various games create a controlled situation where sheer strategy must be used (as in chess), or where strategy combines with persuasion and is tempered by luck (as in *Monopoly*). Fantasy, likewise, isolates and highlights elements of our world. *Grimm's Tales* often turn on the keeping or breaking of a promise (as in *The Frog Prince* or *Beauty and the Beast*).

---

19   Ibid., 146.
20   Caillois, "The Definition of Play, The Classification of Games," 128.

The tales of Arthur's knights often underline the virtues (or vices) of the round table heroes, helping us see again the importance of character. Very, very often, however, fairy tales draw our attention again to the natural world: helping us see animals by making them talk, helping us feel the wildness of the weather through out-of-door adventures, or simply by reminding us of the 'mood' of certain times of day.

This same desire to "give back to us" our own experience seems to be present in the artistry of Miyamoto. A recent *New Yorker* piece writes,

> In his games, Miyamoto has always tried to re-create his childhood wonderment, if not always the actual experiences that gave rise to it, since the experiences themselves may be harder to come by in a paved and partitioned world. "I can still recall the kind of sensation I had when I was in a small river, and I was searching with my hands beneath a rock, and something hit my finger, and I noticed it was a fish," he told me one day. "That's something that I just can't express in words. It's such an unusual situation. I wish that children nowadays could have similar experiences, but it's not very easy."[21]

§9 Tolkien's final necessary condition for a fairy tale is the joyful, consoling ending of the tale.

> But the "consolation" of fairy-tales has another aspect than the imaginative satisfaction of ancient desires. Far more important is the Consolation of the Happy Ending. Almost I would venture to assert that all complete fairy-stories must have it. At least I would say that Tragedy is the true form of Drama, its highest function; but the opposite is true of Fairy-story.[22]

---

21 "The Master of Play," *New Yorker*, 88.
22 Tolkien, "On Fairy Stories," 153.

The happy ending of fairy tales Tolkien christens "eucatastrophe" (or, a "good" catastrophe). This sudden "joyous turn" is what we find at the end of so many beloved fairy stories. Cinderella gets to go to the ball when the fairy godmother appears. The frog prince dies and is returned to human form. The woodcutter appears and saves Red Riding Hood.

This consoling turn satisfies because it is happy, but also because it is miraculous. It is, in a sense, a "deus ex machina" ending. It provides an escape from the sadness of our own world by way of a kind of divine grace. As Tolkien writes, this happy ending is not mere optimism. It does not say that sorrow and death are unreal. Rather, as Tolkien sees it "the possibility of these [sad events] is necessary to the joy of deliverance." What the eucatastrophe denies is that evil must prevail. In this way, again, fairy stories reflect a deeply Christian hope. Writes Tolkien, "[eucatastrophe] denies (in the face of much evidence, if you will) universal final defeat and in so far is evangelium, giving a fleeting glimpse of Joy, Joy beyond the walls of the world, poignant as grief."[23] The incarnation of Christ was, for Tolkien, the eucatastrophic turn in all of human history. And the resurrection of Christ, as written in the gospels, was the happy ending that changed the tragic meaning of the Messiah's death into something that signified hope and consolation.

In Tolkien's own most popular stories, *The Hobbit* and *The Lord of the Rings*, we find his ideas most clearly embodied. In both stories, what looks like utter disaster is turned into a happy ending suddenly and unexpectedly. In *The Hobbit*, the sudden appearance of the goblins looks like it will destroy the men of Laketown, the wood elves and the dwarves, until the equally sudden appearance of the eagles and Beorn, who turn the tide. Similarly, in *The Lord of the Rings,* Frodo's journey to Mt. Doom ends in seeming defeat, as he cannot bring himself to destroy the ring of power. All seems to be lost, until Gollum bites off Frodo's

---

23   Ibid.

finger and then promptly falls into the volcano. Still, Sam and Frodo are likely to die on Mt. Doom until the eagles, again, save the day and turn their tragic-heroic tale into a much happier one. As in fairy tales and the Christ story, what looks to be destined for doom suddenly and unexpectedly turns to joy.

§9a Without too many conceptual backbends, we can see a connection to the world of fantasy and the world of gaming. Roger Caillois rightly notes that all games are uncertain.[24] Winning or losing is never guaranteed. If it were, there would be no game. Who would play a game they knew they could not win (except, perhaps, if repeated playing enabled one to eventually win)? Who would play a game they knew they could not lose? This would be utterly tedious.

The ending of the game is open. It may end in victory or defeat. To win, then, is always a revelation. It always contains the element of surprise. In this way, too, *The Legend of Zelda* participates in the genre of fairy tale.

§9b After much fighting and struggle, you reach the final dungeon. You die numerous times, as enemies pile on in greater numbers than you have ever before encountered. Each time you die, you are sent back to the beginning of the dungeon and have to fight your way through again. This is frustrating, edging toward tedious, and you begin to worry that, perhaps, you will never complete the game. Then you come upon a new weapon, the silver arrow, which your dog-eared copy of Nintendo Power indicates is necessary for defeating Ganon.

After getting the silver arrow, however, there is more struggle and fighting until you reach the final room, where Ganon is. Though most creatures are only as big as you are, Ganon is at least four times your size. He stands there, a hulking green menace. And then he disappears. This is frustrating. Then fireballs begin to rain down on you from his unseen hands as he moves around the screen. This is profoundly unfair, you feel, and you begin stabbing wildly, hemorrhaging hearts all the while. Finally, you strike him by accident,

---

24   Caillois, "The Definition of Play, The Classification of Games," 128.

The Birth of Gaming from the Spirit of Fantasy

he appears for a moment before disappearing again and the fireballs resume. You die and respawn at the beginning of the level.

Again and again you fight Ganon, only to die. Until one time, on the edge of despair, you manage to stab him again and again, and then again. He ceases to be invisible now and, remembering the silver arrow, you shoot it at him and he explodes into a series of 8-bit fireballs. You advance into the next room and there is Zelda.

You put down your controller, your thumbs aching and your palms sweaty. You have done it. You turn off your NES and go outside to walk around and enjoy the moment. For a little while, you feel certain that anything is possible.

[§10 Essay over, but go to §8d.]

The Legend of Zelda and Theology

Freedom versus Destiny: A Hero's Call

Josh and Rachel Rasmussen

"Among the descendants of the Knights of Hyrule a hero must appear" (Legend of Zelda: A Link to the Past)

Introduction

The future of Hyrule looks grim. The princesses have been captured. Mummies and monsters roam the villages. Ganon's evil schemes to procure the power of the Triforce have almost finished their course — and yet, a sliver of hope remains. According to legend, a heroic warrior would arise at Hyrule's darkest hour to conquer Ganon and restore the Kingdom to its former glory.

Meanwhile, a boy from beyond Faron Woods starts to fight against the spreading corruption. Hyrule takes heart as the bold, young Link defeats monsters one by one and finally comes face to face with Ganon himself.

Princess Zelda assures Link, "You are the legendary hero. I have felt this from the first time we met."[1] With confidence, Link picks up his sword and faces the powerful Tyrant. Link dodges Ganon's attacks and, with a striking blow of his sword, he sends Ganon back into the darkness from whence he came. Peace is restored to the Kingdom and the people praise Link as the Hero of Old.

"But wait a minute," Link thinks to himself, "no ancient Sages ever told me to leave my home to save Hyrule from evil. I *chose* to do that myself! How is it that I am the foretold hero if I could have chosen to stay home and herd goats?" Perplexed, Link is left wondering, "How can a legendary Hero of Old really be free?"

---

1   *The Legends of Zelda: A Link to the Past*. 21 November 1991. (Nintendo). SNES. 30 October 2010.

Link is not the only one who has asked a question like this. Religious thinkers and philosophers throughout the ages have wondered how freedom and destiny might fit together. Is it possible for God, prophets or wizards to predict, and even plan, what someone will *freely* do? If it is truly one's destiny to be a hero, can one resist that destiny? Or do divine forces ensure that foretold heroes stay on their destined paths?

Foretold destinies are not confined to the realm of fantasy. There are several alleged prophecies throughout history that purport to describe the future of mankind. Ancient Hebrew texts, for example, describe a future messiah who would bring salvation to mankind and restore peace to the earth after a time of tribulation and war.[2] But on what basis could prophets predict the fate of mankind? After all, isn't it *up to us* (or, at least to our world leaders) whether or not we go to war? If it *is* up to us, then how could anyone know for sure what kind of future we will choose?

These questions reveal a tension between free will and destiny. This tension can be turned into an objection to all religions that predict the future. The objection is this:

Premise 1: People can make choices.

Premise 2: If people can make choices, then no one can predict the future.

Therefore: Religions that claim to predict the future are false.

If this objection succeeds, then religions relying on prophecy are in jeopardy. So, a lot hinges upon whether or not freedom and destiny can, indeed, be coherently linked together.

Thankfully, philosophers and theologians have developed various accounts of how freedom and destiny might be compatible. In this chapter, we will lay out these accounts and consider whether any of them are plausible.

---

2   See, for example, Jeremiah 23:5, 6; 33, 15, 6; Isaiah 11:10, Zechariah 14:1–9; Ezekiel 38–39.

The "No Solution" Solution

The problem at hand is to understand how anyone could possibly have a foretold destiny if people have genuine free will. The first "solution" is to suppose that there is in fact *no solution* to this problem. In other words, freedom and destiny are *not* compatible. On this view, either no one is free or else there are no foretold destinies (or both).

Consider first the option that no one is free. This means that we don't actually make choices. It may *seem* to you as though you can choose whether or not to continue reading this. But that is an illusion. The truth is that either you *must* continue reading without choosing to do so, or else you *must* stop without choosing to. You lack freedom either way. Call this the No Freedom option.

Hardly anyone would *want* the No Freedom option to be true. It flies in the face of common sense. What's worse is that it seems to imply that no one is ever morally responsible for his or her actions. For how could one be morally responsible for actions that one doesn't freely do? For example, how could you be blamed for stealing a candy bar if you had no choice in the matter? If we lack freedom, then it seems we lack moral responsibility too. Yet, it seems absurd to think that no one is ever morally responsible for one's actions. For this reason, most people (though not all) will likely choose to reject the No Freedom option.

An alternative to the No Freedom option is to think that people simply do not have a "destiny." This is the No Destiny option. With this option, religions that claim to tell the future are in error (and any accurate predictions would be mere coincidence). The future is open-ended and, thus, no one can predict it with absolute certainty.

The basic argument for the No Destiny option is as follows:
Premise 1: People make free choices.
Premise 2: If people make choices, then no one has a destiny that was foretold.
Therefore: No one has a destiny that was foretold.
Almost everyone would grant Premise 1. Most people think that we make

free choices at least *sometimes*. Thus, for most of us, the argument for No Destiny hinges upon Premise 2, which suggests that free choices and foretold destinies are incompatible. The obvious question to ask here is this: why think that freedom and destiny are incompatible?

We will consider the most common—and most powerful—argument for thinking that freedom and destiny are incompatible. The argument, which we will call the Master Argument, is this:

Premise 1: If an action is free, then it doesn't *have to* happen.

Premise 2: If an action is foretold, then it does have to happen.

Therefore: No action is both free *and* foretold.

Premise 3: If no action is both free and foretold, then no free person has a destiny that was foretold.

Therefore: No free person has a destiny that was foretold.

We'll look more closely at the Master Argument throughout the following sections. The remainder of this chapter is devoted to seeing if there is a way to escape this argument.

Compatibilism

Compatibilism is the view that our freedom to choose is compatible with various forces (divine or natural) *necessitating* our actions. In other words, according to the compatibilist, our choices are free even though God or nature set up the world so that we must make the very choices we make.

To clarify this, let us consider an example. Imagine that the three goddesses (the ancient ones who created the Triforce) created a world in which Link finds himself with a sword in his hand and Ganon standing menacingly between himself and Princess Zelda. Now also imagine that the goddesses set up the scenario and designed the psychological makeup of these creatures so that the following sequence of events would ensue: Ganon takes one step forward, Zelda screams and then Link strikes once to the right, once to the left, thrusts his sword into Ganon's side and, finally, rushes to Zelda's rescue.

From the perspective of the characters, their actions accord with what they *want* to do. But from the perspective of the goddesses, it is no surprise how each character acts because each is determined to act in a specified way—right down to the pattern of Link's sword swinging. Thus, the exact same sequence of events would occur if it were replayed a thousand times. We see, then, that according to compatibilism, an omniscient mind might be able to foresee the future by setting up the initial conditions and then calculating which future events will necessarily unfold.

This notion of freedom has an interesting consequence: it implies that an action can be free even if the one performing that action *couldn't have done otherwise*. This consequence suggests a way of reconciling freedom and destiny. Recall Premise 1 of the Master Argument. It says that if an action is free, then it *didn't have to* happen; that is, one *could have* done otherwise. This premise is precisely what compatibilism denies. Therefore, if compatibilism is true, then the Master Argument fails.

Is compatibilism a good move? Is it true? To address these questions, let us think more carefully about what compatibilism implies. Suppose, for the sake of argument, that the first state of the universe necessitates every subsequent state. (If you don't think the universe had a *first* state, just pick some state that occurred eons ago.) Then, a state of the universe in the distant past would necessitate all our present thoughts and actions. Indeed, even your decision to read these very words would ultimately be determined (necessitated) by the initial state of the universe. Compatiblism, therefore, implies that all our decisions would still count as free *even if* they were completely determined by a state of the universe that occurred eons ago. That's certainly a provocative implication.

We can draw this out further. Consider that the first state of the universe is obviously outside your control, as it occurred before you even existed. Also, any *necessary consequences* of something outside your control would seem to be outside your control. It follows, then, that any necessary consequences of the first state of the universe are outside your control. But free actions, by definition, are within your control. Therefore, *if* the first state of the universe ultimately necessitates all future states, then none of your actions are free (because none are within your control). In other words, compatibilism seems to imply something that's false; it seems to imply that your actions could be free even if they were outside your control.

To reply to this, one must explain how a free action could be a necessary consequence of events that occurred eons ago. Such an explanation is not easy to come up with, but I won't say that it cannot be done.

Simple Foreknowledge

In the previous section, we imagined that the three goddesses set up the world to *make* Link thrust his sword into Ganon's side. Now let's imagine that the three goddesses don't set up forces to cause Link to act a certain way. Instead, the goddesses merely *foresee* the free choices that Link will make. Call this the Simple Foreknowledge view.

A challenge for the Simple Foreknowledge view is to explain *how* a being could foreknow events that have yet to happen. We cannot say that a being knows the future merely by carefully calculating what will likely happen. For knowing what will *likely* happen isn't the same as knowing what *will* happen. How, then, can a being know the future?

Theologians have proposed two different hypotheses to answer this deep and difficult question. One hypothesis is that an omniscient being, like God, can observe future events directly. According to this hypothesis, God is not restricted by a perspective in time in the way creatures are. God stands outside of time and, as such, is able to see everything—past, present, and future—*at once*. God knows what will happen in the distant future by *observing* this future from a perspective outside the confines of time. On this scenario, the future is not a necessary consequence of the past. Rather, God simply observes (from a timeless perspective) how everything happens to turn out throughout all time.

This hypothesis depends upon a certain view about the nature

Freedom versus Destiny: A Hero's Call

of time and existence. Specifically, it requires that events that haven't happened yet actually *exist*. For, if future events don't actually exist (but merely *will* exist), then they can't actually be observed—not even by God. Some people may have no problem thinking of future events as existing, but it's worth noting that the question of whether or not future events exist is hotly debated among today's philosophers.[3]

A second hypothesis is that God foreknows the future, not by observation, but by direct insight. This insight is sometimes compared with our memories of the past: just as we can *remember* events that *did* happen, perhaps God is able to *"foremember"* events that *will* happen. On this view, God does not need to observe future events to predict them any more than we need to observe past events to remember them. Thus, this hypothesis allows God to experience our perspective in time but still know the future.

So far, we have considered how an action that doesn't *have to* happen could perhaps be foreknown and so foretold. Given this, one might deny Premise 2 of the Master Argument, which says that if an action is indeed foretold, then it *must* happen.[4] The possibility is open, then, for an action to be both free and foreknown.

However, destiny is more than mere foreknowledge. Destiny includes *purpose* and *planning*. In other words, if someone has a destiny, it

---

[3] For a defense of the view that future events do not exist, see: Craig, William Lane. *Time and Eternity: Exploring God's Relationship to Time*. Crossway Books. 2001. For a defense of the view that they do, see: (Sider, Theodore. *Four-Dimensionalism*. Oxford University Press. 2001.) or (Greene, Brian. *The Fabric of the Cosmos: Space, Time, and the Texture of Reality*. Vintage. 2004.)

[4] When I say that an action "must happen," what I mean is that the action is a necessary *consequence* of past events that cause later events. Someone might have a broader meaning in mind, however—one according to which an action "must happen" if someone simply knows ahead that it will happen. On this understanding of "must happen," the Simple Foreknowledge strategy is actually no threat to Premise 2 of the Master Argument. But it is then a threat to Premise 1. The reason is simple: if free actions can indeed be foreknown in either of the ways I suggested, then any such actions "must happen" (because they are foreknown), which contradicts Premise 1.

is not just *by accident*. For example, if Link's destiny was to defeat Ganon, that's no accident. It's something the goddesses hoped for—indeed, orchestrated. This opens up a deeper challenge: how can free actions be foreknown *and* orchestrated?

Sophisticated Foreknowledge

Some theologians have proposed that God's knowledge can be divided into three layers.[5] In the first layer, God knows all the necessary truths—such as *no square has six sides*, or *prime ministers are not prime numbers*. This is the most fundamental layer of knowledge in God. In the next layer, God knows what every possible being *would freely choose to do* in every possible situation. For example, the goddesses would know what Link would choose to do if he were to see Ganon planting flowers in the royal garden while whistling a happy tune and they would know this *even if* Link will never, in fact, encounter Ganon in the royal garden. The idea, then, is that God knows how people would freely act in any and every possible situation in which they could be. This knowledge provides a foundation for God's decision of what type of a world to make (including *who* to create), which in turn provides a foundation for the third layer in God's knowledge—his foreknowledge of what *will*, in fact, happen. We will call this view the Sophisticated Foreknowledge view.[6]

To illustrate, suppose the goddesses of the Triforce had sophisticated foreknowledge as described above. They then would know what Link and all other possible characters would do in every possible circumstance. For example, they would know what Link and Link's uncle each would freely do if they were independently faced with the task of rescuing the seven princesses. Perhaps Link would choose to rise up in courage to defeat the enemies and save the princesses, whereas Link's

---

5 Flint, Tom. *Divine Providence: The Molinist Account*. Ithaca, New York: Cornell University Press. 1998.
6 Theologians call this view 'Molinism', after the Jesuit philosopher, Luis de Molina.

uncle would choose to respond to danger by guarding others from it and not fighting against it himself. If the goddesses were to know these things, then they could use this knowledge to reach certain goals. For example, the goddesses could, perhaps, make sure that Link, and not his uncle, would eventually gain all the resources and opportunities to save the princesses. They could take into account not only what Link and his uncle would do, but also what each of the enemies would do—how they would fight, etc. Then with careful planning, they could choose to create a sequence of events leading Link to the task, knowing that he would *freely* undertake it and succeed. With the freely chosen future in place, the goddesses can accurately testify to that future with a prophecy of a legendary hero who is to come. (Interestingly, the prophecy itself could be one of the very things that would inspire Link to freely choose his destiny.)

But what happens if Link chooses not to be the legendary hero? Would he, thereby, mess up his destiny? Actually, in that case, the goddesses would have known of Link's lack of heroism ahead of time. Thus, they would not have even *tried* to give Link that destiny. Instead, they presumably would have found someone else to rise up; or, if they foresaw that no one *would* rise up, they simply wouldn't be able to predict a future hero. So, Link's choices make a difference: They determine what the goddesses knew long ago and, thus, they make a difference to what sort of destinies they were able to lay out.

This is certainly a creative solution to the puzzle of free will and destiny. It also has an interesting implication about the nature of the past: it implies that people can affect what God (or goddesses) knew and did *in the past*. For example, if God expresses a prophecy about what will happen in the future and, if this prophecy depends upon what people freely do today, then people presently have the ability to affect whether or not God has *in the past* expressed that very prophecy! Some thinkers have found this implication hard to swallow, while others have viewed it as an avenue toward a deeper and more nuanced understanding of the nature of time.

Limited Foreknowledge

There is another proposal for how to reconcile freedom and destiny. This one denies Premise 3 of the Master Argument, which says that if no free actions are known in advance, then no one has a foretold destiny. Perhaps this can be denied; perhaps there can be a foretold destiny even if no free actions are known in advance.

To illustrate this option, imagine that the goddesses do not know in advance what free choices people will make. So, for example, when the goddesses imparted a portion of their power to the Triforce, they didn't know for certain whether the Sages would be able to guard it throughout all of time. Yet, once they saw that Ganon decided to steal the Triforce, they revealed a prophecy to the Sages that a hero would arise to battle evil and restore the Triforce to its rightful place. The prophecy was not based upon their foresight of what people would freely choose to do; rather, it was based upon their *intent* to protect the Triforce from the schemes of evil creatures. The goddesses, in their wisdom, would decide when and how to intervene to make sure that history would go according to plan.

Now, let's say that Ganon has just stolen a piece of the Triforce. Meanwhile, the goddesses observe that the young boy Link is a good candidate for being the prophesied legendary hero. The goddesses use their power to equip Link with the appropriate tools and motivation to embark on the mission of retrieving the Triforce. Link does not have to fight, though. He could choose to stay home and herd goats. In that case, the goddesses would seek another hero. Let us suppose, however, that Link freely chooses to come into the role of the hero. Even then, he is still free to choose *which path* fulfills his destiny as a hero. For example, he can decide to storm the Ice Palace before entering the Desert Palace, or he can decide to fight all Bush Spiders right-handed.

At some point, the goddesses will make sure that Link continues on his path of destiny, even if this means overriding his free choices. So, for example, if Link decides that he is not brave enough to fight Ganon and forms the intent of running away, the goddesses may choose to impart extra bravery into Link's heart to cause him to continue the fight. There is always the chance that the free agents will not act as expected; in which case, intervention is necessary.

This account faces a challenging question: if God is *omniscient*, as is traditionally thought, then wouldn't God, thereby, know everything about the future? This is relevant to the game of *Zelda*, too, as the goddesses are said to be omniscient.[7] An omniscient being supposedly knows all truths. So, they should know every truth about the future—including truths concerning what people will or will not do. How, then, can we say that the goddesses have *limited* foreknowledge, lacking knowledge of what people will freely do?

Philosophers have developed a couple of proposals. One is to suppose that God should only be expected to know *as much as is possible to know*.[8] It is not possible to know what people will freely do in the future, they say. Therefore, God should not be expected to know what people will freely do in the future. A drawback to this answer is that it gives up the traditional understanding of God as knowing *all* truths. It is also inadequate to *Legend of Zelda* theology, for the goddesses are explicitly said to be omniscient—to know everything.

The other proposal is to suppose that there are simply no truths about what people will freely do. The future is open and unsettled. For example, before Link decided to leave his home to fight Ganon, it was not true that he was going to choose to fight; nor was it true that he was going to choose *not* to fight. Both choices were open and unsettled. Therefore, the goddesses could be omniscient—knowing all truths—and yet still not know with certainty what choices Link would make ahead of time.

---

7   See the introduction story: *The Legends of Zelda: A Link to the Past.* 21 November 1991. (Nintendo). SNES. 30 October 2010.

8   van Inwagen, Peter. "What does an omniscient being know about the future?" in J. Kvanvig (ed.) *Oxford Studies in Philosophy of Religion*, I. Oxford: Oxford University Press. 2008. 216-230.

Some theologians believe that this is precisely how things are with God. God is omniscient and, therefore, knows all truths. But when it comes to truths about what people will freely do, there aren't any such truths to know. On this view, God can still make prophecies and create destinies by *intending* to steer events and creatures toward a desired outcome. Of the views discussed, this view places the most limits on what God knows, but some have considered it to be the most realistic option.

Conclusion

We have laid out several models for how freedom and destiny might be able to fit together. Each has its strengths and weaknesses and, thus, it might seem difficult to figure out which, if any, is the correct one. However, even if we cannot resolve precisely *how* freedom and destiny fit together, we have shown that the union of freedom and destiny might well be perfectly coherent. It remains philosophically possible, then, that prophetic destinies and legendary heroes are more than just fictional elements in the game of *Zelda*.

The Mediation of Transcendence within The Legend of Zelda: The Wind Waker

Mark Hayse

> ...fairy land arouses a longing for he knows not what. It stirs and troubles him (to his life-long enrichment) with the dim sense of something beyond his reach and, far from dulling or emptying the actual world, gives it a new dimension of depth.
>
> C. S. Lewis, "On Three Ways of Writing For Children"[1]

Introduction

My first encounter with *The Legend of Zelda: Wind Waker* immediately struck a chord deep within me. As C. S. Lewis might put it, the game "aroused, stirred, and troubled" me with the "dim sense" of something more—something transcendent. From the Latin *transcendere*, transcendence literally means "to climb beyond." Other games stake their claims upon the terrain of stark realism—simulating real-life processes. However, *Wind Waker* clearly transcends (or climbs beyond) the literalistic conventions of sports, military and life simulations. The "fairy land" of *Wind Waker* playfully mediates an experience of "something beyond the player's reach"—mystery and wonder, the stuff of transcendence.

We can experience the spirit of transcendence across many aspects of culture, even its non-religious aspects. The classical symphonies of Brahms, Beethoven or Bartok evoke a yearning and longing that soar above daily life. The lights, sounds and images

---

[1] Lewis, Clive Staples. (1982). *On stories, and other essays on literature*, ed. Walter Hooper. New York, NY: Harcourt Brace Jovanovich.

at a U2 arena concert routinely approach the level of liturgy. The historic folklore of *Grimm's Fairy Tales* or the *Tales of the Arabian Nights* pull readers into whole worlds beyond normal reach. Likewise, the contemporary pulp fiction of H. P. Lovecraft or Robert E. Howard draws readers' imaginations into wonder and amazement. In Barcelona, Spain, the physical architecture of Antoni Gaudi's *Sagrada Família* hypnotizes visitors with its playful synthesis of faith and fantasy. Similarly, the digital architecture of Shigeru Miyamoto's *Wind Waker* enchants players with its fairyland of transcendence. All forms of culture—including the digital—can mediate transcendence by enchanting daily life with a touch of magic.

This essay analyzes the various ways in which *Wind Waker* playfully mediates transcendence. When analyzing video games, careful research requires the consideration of multiple approaches. For example, Frans Mäyrä[2] divides this task into three domains: humanities (literature, philosophy, art), social science (psychology, sociology, anthropology), and design (industry benchmarks, program logic, player experience). On one hand, Marie Laure-Ryan[3] and Janet Murray[4] argue that the analysis of video games should focus on their story qualities. In contrast, Jesper Juul[5] and Ian Bogost[6] analyze video games in terms of structures, procedures and rules. Thus, this essay will analyze transcendence in *Wind Waker* from aesthetic, narrative and procedural perspectives—not so much in terms of theological *formulation* as theological *mediation*.

---

2 Mäyrä, Frans. (2008). *An introduction to game studies: Games in culture.* London: SAGE Publications.

3 Ryan, Marie-Laure. (2001). Beyond myth and metaphor: The case of narrative in digital media. *Game Studies* 1, no. 1. http://www.gamestudies.org/0101/ryan/ (accessed July 16, 2011).

4 Murray, Janet. (2005). The last word on ludology v narratology in game studies. Paper at Digital Games Research Association Conference (DiGRA 2005), Vancouver, Canada, June 17, 2005. http://www.lcc.gatech.edu/~murray/digra05/lastword.pdf (accessed July 16, 2011).

5 Juul, Jesper. (2005). *Half-real: Video games between real rules and fictional worlds.* Cambridge, MA: MIT Press.

6 Bogost, Ian. (2006). *Unit operations: An approach to videogame criticism.* Cambridge, MA: MIT Press.

The Mediation of Transcendence within The Legend of Zelda: The Wind Waker

Aesthetic Perspectives on Transcendence in Wind Waker

The visual aesthetic of *Wind Waker* mediates transcendence in a variety of ways, beginning with the game box cover art and the game's opening moments. The cover art appears quite plain at first glance. It flatly depicts a side view of the King of Red Lions (the hero's talking ship) accompanied by the words "Wind Waker" in a quasi-Celtic script. However, the cover art presents more than immediately meets the eye. Faintly embossed upon the plain background is a three-dimensional image of Link (the hero) sailing the seas upon the King of Red Lions. Together, they ride the crest of a crashing wave, almost leaping off of the game box. Wide-eyed with wonder and smiling with delight, Link gazes off toward horizons unknown. A bright sunburst fills the sky behind him. Link anticipates something greater to come, as does the player.

Similarly, the game's opening moments begin with a deceptively simple sequence. The camera looks up into a bright blue sky. The sun shines brightly. Sea winds blow as a sailor's shanty plays. Waves crash and seagulls fly as the camera pans across Outset Island—Link's home. Soon, the camera finds Link standing alone on a high cliff's edge, wind blowing in his hair, gazing out across the mysterious sea. In both the cover art and the opening sequence, Link senses a deep longing for adventure that infects the player as well.

Wind Waker's visual aesthetic of transcendence also appears in its visual effects. Its three-dimensional, cel-shaded artistry far more resembles a Disney/Pixar feature film than a photorealistic sports game or symbolic puzzle game. *Wind Waker* introduces the use of the yellow C-Stick as a new way to explore its magical terrain. By moving the C-Stick, the player moves the camera and changes perspective in all directions. For the first time, this grants fully panoramic views of Hyrule's fantasy landscape. Thus, the sensation of entering *Wind Waker's* Hyule is like Dorothy's transition from the gray world of her Kansas home into the Technicolor Land of Oz. This combination of three-dimensional cel-shading and panoramic visual access visually immerses the player in *Wind Waker's* fairy land.

Wind Waker's visual effects also communicate magic and wonder. In the forest, the hazy air flickers with the soft glow of fireflies. Similarly, delicate snowflakes silently fall all around as the player explores islands made of ice. Within fiery caverns, bubbling lava pops and flows underfoot. Raging sea storms enclose the player with clouds and lightning. Mighty cyclones tower into the sky, their chaotic peaks beyond the range of sight. When treasure chests open, brilliant shafts of light burst forth. Comforting wisps of wind gently curl and blow across the sea. Titanic fairies rise from the waves, laughing and blowing shimmering translucent petals upon Link. Link also confronts colossal boss monsters, truly terrifying to behold—Gohma, an enormous volcanic scorpion; Molgera, a gigantic sand worm; and Big Octo, a tentacled leviathan. In all of these contexts, *Wind Waker* plunges the player into a world of wondrous images that transcend ordinary life.

Even the arrangement of *Wind Waker's* musical aesthetic supports a mood of transcendent anticipation. As the game begins at Outset Island, the music enters with light, hushed tones. Flutes and violins play crisp, repeating, two-note phrases. Clarinets and oboes answer in kind, more strongly. Throughout this chapter, the melody never fully resolves into its tonic chord—the triad of notes which brings completion and finality. The combined effect produces a feeling of musical tiptoeing and childlike wonder. Each musical device builds a sense of anticipation for something more to come. Likewise, the theme song of the Great Sea never resolves into the tonic, evoking a mood of adventure. The Great Sea theme begins with the crash of a cymbal as ocean spray splashes over the ship's bow. Waves of trombones and cellos imitate the sound and rhythm of the rolling sea. The snare drum snaps a crisp, marching cadence. The Great Sea Theme is much firmer than the Outset Island theme, filling the player's heart with boldness as Link sets sail for undiscovered country. Finally, the End Credits theme intertwines various melodies and themes into a single, coherent conversation

The Mediation of Transcendence within The Legend of Zelda: The Wind Waker

through point and counterpoint. This final theme evokes transcendence through a musical synthesis in which many voices become one. As each voice adds its own accent and depth, an unexpected singularity emerges that beautifully unites it all. Interestingly, this process is vividly illustrated in the online work of FreddeGredde,[7] an Internet musician whose "Wind Waker Unplugged" received over three million YouTube hits in less than three years. His arrangement of the End Credits theme demonstrates the way in which many voices can work together to produce something greater than the sum of their parts.

In summary, the various visual and musical aspects of *Wind Waker* combine to mediate an aesthetic of transcendence. The game box and cover art suggest a greater mystery within. The opening moments suggest distant horizons yet undiscovered. The visual artistry conjures a sense of transport into fairylands otherwise inaccessible. Throughout game play, the music teases the player with a sense of anticipation realized, at last, only during the End Credits.

Narrative Perspectives on Transcendence in Wind Waker

  C. S. Lewis and J. R. R. Tolkien associate story with transcendence throughout their literary and religious works. Tolkien maintains that the "imaginative inventions" of fantasy originate with God, "reflecting a splintered fragment of the true light."[8] Like Tolkien, Lewis argues that "myth is the isthmus which connects the peninsular world of thought with that vast continent we really belong to."[9] Both

---

7 Larsson, Fredrik. (2008, December 24). Wind Waker unplugged (FreddeGredde) [Video file]. http://www.youtube.com/watch?v=uRv8gnBMiWM (accessed July 16, 2011).

8 Carpenter, Humphrey. (1979). *The inklings: C. S. Lewis, J. R. R. Tolkien, Charles Williams, and their friends.* Boston, MA: Houghton Mifflin, 43.

9 Lewis, Clive Staples. (1970). *God in the dock: Essays on theology and ethics.* Grand Rapids, MI: Eerdmans, 67.

mythmakers believe that the power of fairy tales hinges upon their ability to reflect something eternal. Lewis describes this feeling as *sehnsucht*—a German compound word for transcendence that defies easy definition. *Sehnsucht* indicates a deep longing or yearning for something elusive and heavenly.[10] Lewis knew *sehnsucht* in his own longing for God, his yearning for love and his paradoxical homesickness for a world of fairies and fantasy. Lewis scholar Corbin Scott Cornell summarizes *sehnsucht* in this way:

> That we have appetites suggests that we will find food. That we get drowsy suggests that sleep exists. That we respond to melody suggests that men will devise music. That we are haunted by unquenchable longings points to a goal for that longing—in eternity if not in time...
> The Well at the World's End, the Green Hills Beyond, Shangri-La, El Dorado, Narnia—Lewis believes these are all splashes of Godlight in the dark wood of our life.

Lewis, Tolkien and Cornell suggest that realms of imagination reflect our innate human longing for something *more*—a transcendent destiny which is our eternal home.

Wind Waker begins with a backstory of *sehnsucht*. A harpsichord and woodwind ensemble plays as the tale unfolds. Woodprint pages scroll across the player's view, annotated in mystic script. Hyrule, once a prosperous and beautiful land, now suffers under oppression and evil. A violin punctuates the tale as a young hero in green appears. Although the hero banishes the evil one, evil returns once again. Its dark eyes fill the skies as cities burn. The people of Hyrule cry out for the hero's return, yearning for salvation. This tale ends upon a Picardy third—the shift from a minor (sad) to a major (happy) chord—representing the light

---

10   Cornell, Scott Carnell. (1974). *Bright shadow of reality: C. S. Lewis and the feeling intellect.* Grand Rapids, MI: Eerdmans.

of hope amidst the dark of despair. Both musically and narratively, the backstory sets the stage for *sehnsucht*.

As chapter one begins, a great bird abducts Link's little sister Ayrll. She quickly becomes a prisoner of the evil Ganon in his Forsaken Fortress. Soon after, the King of Red Lions offers assistance to Link. Eyes wide with wonder, Link grasps the Wind Waker—an elemental baton that enables its user to control the wind. Wind Waker in Link's hand, the player sets sail across an expansive ocean world to rescue Ayrll, restore wisdom and defeat evil once again. Along the way, the player meets ethereal spirits, mysterious gods and elemental forces. Link discovers and explores dozens of mysterious islands, quaint villages, hidden temples and cavernous dungeons. Ultimately, the game's story takes on an epic scope that involves persistent hope, family reunion, redemption throughout the land and the restoration of all things. The *Wind Waker* is a story of longing, shared in a unique way by both Link and the player.

Video game theorists argue that players view their onscreen avatars as extensions of themselves. For example, MIT psychologist Sherry Turkle[11] contends that video games provide players with playful environments in which to explore various aspects of their own personalities. Similarly, researcher James Paul Gee describes this unique relationship between self and avatar in terms of *projective identity*. Gee's notion of projective identity plays on two senses of the word "project"—not only "to project one's values and desires onto the virtual character" but also to see "the virtual character as one's own project in the making."[12] The heroes of film and literature act independently of the audience. In video games, however, the player enjoys a very active role

---

11   Turkle, Sherry. (1995). *Life on the screen: Identity in the age of the internet.* New York: Simon & Schuster. (2005). *The second self: Computers and the human spirit*, 20th anniversary ed. Cambridge, MA: MIT Press.

12   (2007). *What video games have to teach us about learning and literacy* (revised and updated edition). New York: Palgrave Macmillan, 50.

in the hero's life.[13] Thus, Gee muses that "The power of video games is not in losing ourselves, but in finding a new being, neither real nor virtual, a blended, fused being."[14] In *Wind Waker*, the player grows and develops as Link does. First, the player transcends his physical body in order to identify with Link. Second, the player participates in the ongoing transformation of Link throughout the game. Third, the player's knowledge and skill grow ever greater. In these ways, the experience of Link and the player can be described as a shared journey of self-transcendence. In fact, Link's very name implies the establishment of a "link" between the player and the avatar.[15]

Joseph Campbell—a twentieth century mythologist—contends that mythical stories best capture the journey of self-transcendence. In particular, Campbell argues that the so-called monomyth of the Hero's Journey best reflects the journey of self-transcendence:

> The standard path of the mythological adventure of the hero is a magnification of the formula represented in the rites of passages: separation—initiation—return: which might be named the nuclear unit of the monomyth.
>
> A hero ventures forth from the world of common day into a region of supernatural wonder: fabulous forces are there encountered and a decisive victory is won: the hero comes back from this mysterious adventure with the power to bestow boons on his fellow man.[16]

---

13   Gee, James Paul. (2005). *Why video games are good for your soul: Pleasure and learning*. Altona, Australia: Common Ground Publishing, 115-116.

14   Gee, James Paul. (2005). *Why video games are good for your soul: Pleasure and learning*. Altona, Australia: Common Ground Publishing, 81.

15   Compagno, Dario. (2008). I am Link's transcendental will: Freedom from Hyrule to Earth. In *The Legend of Zelda and philosophy: I Link therefore I am*, ed. Luke Cuddy, 179-189. Chicago, IL: Open Court, 181.

16   Campbell, Joseph. (1962). *The hero with a thousand faces*. Cleveland, OH: World Publishing, 30.

The Mediation of Transcendence within The Legend of Zelda: The Wind Waker

Campbell also maintains that the happy ending of the monomyth points to "a transcendence of the universal tragedy of man."[17] In other words, the monomyth tells the story of a hero overcoming suffering, pain and even death. The self-transcendence monomyth underpins many myths, not only those of formal religion but also those of popular culture.

In *Wind Waker,* both Link and the player begin the game with little more than a yearning for adventure. Link possesses no skills, no tools and no distinction of any kind. Over time, Link comes to master a sword. He learns to slice, to thrust, to spin, to parry. Link gains the power to defeat ever-stronger enemies. He gathers hearts of strength which sustain him when attacked. He accumulates wealth, wisdom and relics of legend. With the Deku Leaf, Link can hang glide to otherwise inaccessible locations. With the Grappling Hook and Hookshot, he gains the ability to swing and climb to remote ledges normally out of reach. Iron Boots enable him to withstand gale-force winds. Power Bracelets grant him the strength to lift a boulder as lightly as a feather. And on Link's journey of self-transcendence, he gains not only ability but also significance. Allies rally around him. Mentors offer guidance and insight. Slowly, Link comes to realize that he is Hyrule's only hope. Once, he was merely a boy. In the end, he embraces his true nature as the Hero of Time born anew. Similarly, the player begins *Wind Waker* as a novice, but ends as an expert. That is why Link can become something *more* only if the player does too. Both Link and the player must become the Hero of Time together. Their shared journey of self-transcendence is intertwined in every chapter of the game.

---

17   Campbell, Joseph. (1962). *The hero with a thousand faces.* Cleveland, OH: World Publishing, 28.

Procedural Perspectives on Transcendence in Wind Waker

Video game scholar and designer Ian Bogost argues that "procedurality" defines the computer medium.[18] Put another way, Bogost understands that video games "require user action to complete their procedural representations."[19] Video game programs consist of procedural rules for play. For example, many video games rely upon the procedural rules of movement, item collection, inventory management, attack and defense. Players bring video game programs to life by putting those procedural rules into action. In fact, Bogost argues that "the most important moment of study" of a video game is the experience of putting procedures into action.[20] The most important procedures in *Wind Waker* are the exploration and navigation of game space.

Wind Waker tantalizes the player with transcendence in its procedures of exploration and navigation. Throughout the game, the player visits wondrous sites normally off-limits to daily life. He climbs dizzying heights, sails to far-off horizons and plumbs cavernous dungeons. The player also realizes that many visible sites cannot be reached immediately, even in the first moments of the game. On Outset Island, *Wind Waker* teases the player with the lure of rupee jewels just out of reach and distant plateaus not readily gained. Once again, this feeds the player's sense of longing for something more. *Wind Waker* allows Link to reach these sites only by escaping his own body. By placing a Hyoi Pear on his head, Link can attract and control a passing seagull, projecting his consciousness into the bird. In seagull mode, the player flies unencumbered to literally gain a bird's eye perspective on otherwise

---

18 Bogost, Ian. (2007). *Persuasive games: The expressive power of videogames.* Cambridge, MA: MIT Press, 4.

19 Bogost, Ian. (2007). *Persuasive games: The expressive power of videogames.* Cambridge, MA: MIT Press, 45.

20 Bogost, Ian. (2006). *Unit operations: An approach to videogame criticism.* Cambridge, MA: MIT Press, 99; cf. 2006, 131.

The Mediation of Transcendence within The Legend of Zelda: The Wind Waker

secret places. This procedure allows Link to collect rupee jewels and to scout sites otherwise hidden from view. On a distant plateau at Outset Island, a giant stone head conceals the entrance to the deepest dungeon in Hyrule. Link initially discovers this plateau in seagull mode during *Wind Waker's* first chapter. However, he cannot reach this site until midway through the game. It takes that long to locate the Deku Leaf and the Power Bracelets that allow him to hang glide to the plateau and lift the stone head. This elusive goal is only one of many that lure the player toward ongoing discovery and exploration of the unknown—a procedure that mediates the call of transcendence.

    Wind Waker also introduces the telescope—a new innovation in the *Zelda* series that also supports the procedure of exploration. As the game begins, Link's little sister Aryll searches Outset Island high and low with her telescope. She looks for Link because the time has come to celebrate his birthday. Aryll discovers him sweetly sleeping atop the lookout tower, lulled to sleep by the sound of lapping waves. Awakening her big brother, she presents him with her telescope as a birthday gift. The telescope magnifies distant images from one to nine times closer. It provides much greater clarity than that allowed by the naked eye. It allows the player to spy upon distant islands and landforms, 360 degrees in every direction. Most importantly, its very existence suggests that that the player should seek the promise of future horizons amidst his present limitations. It is a symbol and tool of transcendence.

    The procedure of exploration finds its fullest expression upon the Great Sea in *Wind Waker*. The Wind Waker baton allows Link to direct music that controls the wind—a handy skill to possess if you want to sail east, but the wind currently blows west. Baton in hand and sail raised, Link eventually discovers a dazzling array of distant islands, hidden coves, sunken treasures and other surprises. These sites remain blank upon the player's sea charts until discovered, stirring the player with the lure of mystery. Interestingly, the game designer limits and orders which islands can be discovered. In this way, the game designer virtually plays a divine role in *Wind Waker*. Link and the player can only proceed according to the game designer's pace and plan. Their longing for adventure and discovery are limited by the designer's will. Elsewhere, I describe this process in terms of *unfolding revelation*—the incremental unveiling of space, story, meaning and purpose in a video game.[21]

In short, the procedures of exploration and discovery in *Wind Waker* both arouse and satisfy the player's longing for transcendent mystery. The game consistently reveals just enough to move ahead, but not as much as the player wishes. This mystery keeps the player pressing on with a hunger to discover more. Gradually, the player uncovers previously hidden areas. However, each new conquest also brings the irony of new mystery. The introduction of the telescope intensifies this experience. It amplifies not only the player's perception but also the player's desire to know more. Religious educator Dwayne Huebner once argued that effective education is "the lure of the transcendent"—an open invitation to go "beyond ourselves" in order to "become what we are not."[22] In my experience, even the imaginary shores of Hyrule lure a player toward transcendent horizons in search of the unknown.

Conclusion

> Now faith is the substance of things hoped for,
> the evidence of things not seen.
>
> (Hebrews 11:1, KJV)

---

21   Hayse, Mark. (2010). Ultima IV: Simulating the religious quest. In *Halos and avatars: Playing video games with God*, ed. Craig Detweiler, 34-36, Louisville, KY: Westminster/John Knox Press.

22   Huebner, Dwayne. ([1985] 1999). Religious metaphors in the language of education. In *The lure of the transcendent: Collected essays by Dwayne E. Huebner*. Edited by Vicki Hillis, 358-368. Collected and introduced by William F. Pinar. Mahwah, NJ: Lawrence Erlbaum, 360-361.

According to director J. J. Abrams,[23] mystery constitutes the heart and soul of transcendence. In his online TED talk, Abrams recounts his early fascination with how things worked beneath the surface and behind the scenes. During a childhood trip to Lou Tannen's Magic Shop, he purchased a "Magic Mystery Box" that promised fifty dollars worth of magic for only fifteen dollars. Abrams still owns this box and he shows it to the audience during his talk. Enigmatically, the box displays a large question mark on the front. More mysteriously still, it remains unopened. Abrams explains:

> I bought this decades ago ... If you look at this, you'll see it's never been opened. But I've had this forever ... Why have I not opened this? And why have I kept it? ... I haven't opened it because it represents something important ... infinite possibility. It represents hope. It represents potential ... I find myself drawn to infinite possibility, that sense of potential. And I realize that mystery is the catalyst for imagination ... maybe there are times when mystery is more important than knowledge ... what are stories but mystery boxes?[24]

Even a casual examination of Abrams' work reveals an affinity for mystery at its core: Layers of intrigue in the television series *Alias*, the elusive meaning of the Island in the television series *LOST*, the obscure origin and fleeting appearance of the monster in the motion

---

23 Abrams, J.J. (2009). J. J. Abrams on the magic of mystery. *Wired* 17(05). http://www.wired.com/techbiz/people/magazine/17-05/mf_jjessay (accessed July 23, 2011).

24 Abrams, J. J. (2008, January). J. J. Abrams' mystery box [Video file]. http://www.ted.com/talks/lang/eng/j_j_abrams_mystery_box.html (accessed July 23, 2011).

picture *Cloverfield*. Abrams' mystery box is analogous to the idea of transcendence. Underneath an ordinary wrapper lies the promise of magic and wonder, temporarily hidden from sight. Someone has placed something beyond reach, behind the veil, awaiting discovery. In my experience, playing *Wind Waker* is like unwrapping the layers of the mystery box . . . at least, until the end of the game.

I never finished *Wind Waker*. Once victory came within reach and I reached the final chapter, I simply quit playing the game altogether. In this, I am not alone.[25] I lost interest once all the nooks and crannies of Hyrule were revealed. My sense of wonder and exhilaration gave way to boredom and disinterest. The joy of exploration faded before the tedium of running errands, gathering every last rupee and trolling for each hidden treasure chest in all forty-nine sectors of the Great Sea. It ruins the magic when no secrets remain. As Lewis points out in the quotation at the beginning of this essay, we cannot separate the joy of fairyland from the experience of longing.

The transcendent heart and soul of *Wind Waker* is mystery, not mastery. Too many video games present problems to solve rather than potentialities to savor. Enchantment is lost amidst its revealing. Once the mystery box is unwrapped, it's only a matter of time until faith becomes sight and tragically obsolete. *Wind Waker* is no exception, although it does a better job than many other games. Its gradually unfolding journey into mystery mediates a transcendent taste of *sehnsucht*, deep calling unto deep (Psalm 42:7), a pop culture foreshadowing of something more ... our true and eternal home.

---

25 Fellela, Toni. (2008). Link's search for meaning. In *The Legend of Zelda and philosophy: I Link therefore I am*, ed. Luke Cuddy, 45-54. Chicago, IL: Open Court.

Take Your Time, Hurry Up, The Choice is Yours: Death and the Afterlife in *The Legend of Zelda: Majora's Mask*

Josh Corman

Part 1: Link's Adventure(s in the "Middle Stage")

Video games are not usually conducive to discussion of the hereafter. Once "Game Over," those two grim words feared by every gamer, appear onscreen, the only option is to restart, buoyed by the knowledge that previous mistakes can be undone. In the next life, we will pilot our avatars to make better decisions, defeat enemies more efficiently and reach his or her highest goals. In this way, because there is traditionally no true death for our main characters in video games,[1] they typically offer us little to no insight into the vast unknown of the afterlife.

Leave it to Shigeru Miyamoto to break the mold. Miyamoto, creator of several of Nintendo's best-loved characters and series (*Mario, Donkey Kong, Starfox,* and *The Legend of Zelda* series, among them), always seems to bring a visionary's appetite for the novel idea to every game with which he is involved. This appetite is apparent in perhaps no game as is it is in *The Legend of Zelda: Majora's Mask*, released in 2000 on the Nintendo 64 gaming system. Though *Majora's Mask* stuck to the same dungeon-crawling formula that had garnered high praise for the *Zelda* franchise, the game is different in a number of ways, from its imposing "three days to save the world" framework, to its alternative location (Termina instead of familiar Hyrule) and its darker, more philosophically engaging storyline.

Specifically, *Majora's Mask* takes a complex and intriguing view of the soul and its relationship to death and the afterlife. Link's adventure in Termina, inadvertently or not, often mirrors the Christian

---

1 While this remains true for the most part, games like *Heavy Rain* and *Mass Effect* are beginning to reshape even this aspect of the medium.

connection between soul and self. For our purposes, we will focus on how *Majora's Mask* treats the soul's passage into the afterlife, its journey through sanctification and its reunification with a spiritually and physically restored body. We also will note the areas in which the game offers a markedly divergent theological perspective from Christianity or simply leaves certain theological questions unaddressed.

Even years after the game's release, it is *Majora's Mask*'s darker, more serious-minded story for which it continues to stand out. Link, our trusty hero from adventures past, is lured into an alternate world – Termina – which resembles his own in some ways, but is ultimately unfamiliar to him. In Termina, Link is faced with two major crises. The first involves the world's impending destruction due to a rapidly approaching (and menacing-looking) moon, which will collide with Termina in three days. The mischievous, mysterious Skull Kid steals Majora's Mask and creates the second crisis, wreaking havoc among the inhabitants of Termina with the powers it has granted him. Luckily (or, perhaps, unluckily) for Link, both of these crises can be resolved upon completion of the same quest, which sees him literally awaken sleeping giants in time to halt the moon's progress with their ancient strength, leaving time to find the Skull Kid and return to life in Hyrule.

Link's hunt for the Skull Kid, and the adventures that this hunt necessitates, will be our primary focus. It is this part of the story that investigates the soul's sanctification after death, its journey toward reunification with a perfected body and its arrival in a place of everlasting reward. To examine *Majora's Mask*'s view on the combination of these subjects, a basic understanding of the Christian view of the soul is necessary. The soul is referenced throughout scripture as that part of the self that is eternal and contains and reveals our consciousness. Genesis 2:7[2] states that when God breathed life into the

---

2   "And the LORD God formed man of the dust of the ground, and breathed into his nostrils the breath of life; and man became a living soul." – *Holy Bible: New International Version (NIV)*.

Take Your Time, Hurry Up, The Choice is Yours

dust of the earth, man was made into a living soul. This verse highlights the fact that human beings, though fully physical, are not merely physical. They are spiritual beings and, indeed, in traditional Christian theology, the soul will continue to live in the intermediate state between death and resurrection,[3] although as an incomplete person. It is the body-soul unity that constitutes human beings as originally created and as fully redeemed after the resurrection.

Majora's Mask takes a similar, but not identical, view of the soul. Darmani the Goron and Mikau the Zora – two characters whom Link aids during his adventures - illustrate that even in Termina the soul is clearly separate from the material body and the soul carries into the afterlife. The game goes much farther than acknowledging the soul's existence or even its condition. Link's adventure is a narrative wherein death is not the end of being and the soul undergoes a type of moral growth and reaches an improved state, similar to the theology of sanctification towards eternal perfection.

The first clue we have that *Majora's Mask* is determined to do more than lead us on a typical adventure is Link's unceremonious alteration into a nameless Deku scrub by the Skull Kid at the game's outset. From that transformation, it is clear that Link enters a different plane, marked most prominently by his long fall into a seemingly endless abyss while chasing the Skull Kid. When Deku Link revives, he is in an unfamiliar place, his trusty horse is gone and the only being he knows in this new land Termina[4] is one of the two fairies who, along with the Skull Kid, accosted him and left him in his miserable state. When Link falls into that dark pit and awakens on an alternate plane, in an altered form, he has, for all intents and purposes, left the world

---

[3] Resurrection particularly pertains to the body in traditional thought. It is not mere resuscitation, but rather a reunion of body and soul that raises the *complete* person to the life of immortality. See I Corinthians 15:35-5

[4] Termina's very name connotes the end (as in terminate), and passage between places (terminal).

behind and emerged into a new existence.

So then, if Termina is the marker of a new existence, or possibly even a realm of the afterlife, of what significance is that realm? Simply put, if Hyrule is a representation of the material world and Termina a representation of an afterworld, is Termina heaven? Hell? Neither? And what exactly is going on there? An examination into what actually happens in Termina and what purposes the events there serve, both for Link and the numerous non-playable characters (NPCs) he encounters, is necessary if we are to establish a working point of view for the discussion of the afterlife and its significance in *Majora's Mask*.

The short answer is that, through Link's encounters in Termina, he accomplishes two primary tasks not related to saving the world. The first deals with others, specifically, providing aid to the spirits of two dead characters. After Link breaks the Skull Kid's initial curse and returns to his natural form, his chase leads him into encounters with the spirits of Darmani, a goron, and Mikau, a Zoran guitarist.

Link's quest leads him to a cave high above Goron Village, snow-covered home to a breed of large, of rock-dwelling creatures, where he meets the disembodied soul of a former Goron tribal leader, Darmani. Darmani has watched helplessly as his village and his people freeze in the grip of a fierce, perpetual winter. While attempting to investigate the source of this trouble, Darmani is blown into a canyon by high winds and killed. In death, he is powerless to help his people and feels tremendous guilt at his inability, despite being one of the wisest and strongest of his people, to save the gorons from destruction. Link proves himself worthy of the appointed task and, after "healing" Darmani's soul with the "Song of Healing," receives a goron mask that turns him instantly into Darmani (or, at least, an approximation close enough to fool the gorons who knew Darmani in life). While wearing the mask, Link embodies Darmani's soul, which, thanks to Link's "healing," has been released from the torment and guilt that kept him trapped in an undefined and helpless "spirit-state." Through his inhabitation of Link,

Darmani is able to re-enter the material world and complete the task that he had failed to accomplish in his own life. In this way, Link serves as a conduit through which the wrongs of Darmani's life could be made right.

This process is, to be sure, a type of sanctification. In Christian theology, sanctification is the process by which the soul is purified from a state of shortcoming and sin to a state of righteousness by God's grace and human acceptance and pursuit of that grace through faith.[5] In simpler terms, theologian H. Ray Dunning defines sanctification as the "renewal of our souls after the image of God."[6] Though Darmani's sanctification is not purification of the spirit in opposition to sin, *per se*, it is the correction and completion of a failed enterprise, the repair of his life's shortcomings, significant to the character's attainment of a greater moral perfection.

Darmani, a warrior-chief who feels that he has failed his people, has guilt that haunts him into the afterlife. His people have been cast into a seemingly eternal winter (much like Narnia's in *The Lion, the Witch, and the Wardrobe*). Darmani dies in an attempt to restore order to his people and mourns his failure in death. As he puts it, "I am dead, but I cannot rest." When Link heals his sorrows, Darmani is shown with a crowd of gorons at his feet, cheering him with raised arms. He says he can feel his sorrows melting away into Link's song. Then, critically, Link's face is superimposed upon Darmani's for a brief moment just before a series of glittering particles, which seem to represent Darmani's spirit, are carried away to compose the goron mask that allows Link to take Darmani's

---

5   Jerry L. Walls. "Purgatory for Everyone." *First Things*. 122 (2002): 26-30

As Walls points out, "...our transformation must be a cooperative venture." He notes his skepticism of a theology whereby God unilaterally and instantaneously sanctifies and justifies us at the moment of death.

6   From Dunning's *Grace, Faith, and Holiness*, Chapter 15: "Sanctification: Renewal in the Image of God"

form. The image of Link's and Darmani's united faces indicates that the mask is not simply a piece of ordinary *Legend of Zelda* magic, but that Link is inhabited by Darmani's spirit itself when he wears that mask. As such, he is able to carry on, doing in life what Darmani could not, and so freeing his soul from its tormented state in the afterlife. Darmani's life is fulfilled in a way, sanctified by Link's intercession.

The sanctification is made complete not when Darmani's spirit is released into the mask, but when Link emerges from Snowhead Temple after defeating one of the pesky evil beings causing problems for the citizens of Termina. When Link returns to the mountain village, spring has finally arrived and brought with it all of the old symbols for rebirth and new life. The eradication of winter is vital because the perfection of Darmani's intentions is made real, creating a corrected, or purified, existence through Link's efforts.

What then, in theological terms, might we come to understand in light of Darmani's situation? Certainly, we can draw one conclusion: in the view of *Majora's Mask*, the end of life is in no way the end of the spirit and, in this case, is no end of the spirit's potential for improvement and purification. In short, Darmani's spirit participates (for lack of a better term) in sanctification after death. Many Christians (typically, though not exclusively, Catholics) couch these thoughts in the language and ideas of purgatory.

Many Roman Catholics hold that purgatory is "a place of temporal punishment for individuals who have not sufficiently repented before death."[7] Though this view is likely more commonly known, for our purposes, an Eastern Orthodox purgatorial theology is perhaps more helpful. Many Eastern theologians view purgatory as a growth process, whereby those who have intellectually assented to faith and begun the process of sanctification complete that process in a temporal realm after death.[8] That the shortcomings of life might be righted through a process

---

7   Jerry L. Walls. "Purgatory for Everyone." *First Things*. 122 (2002): 26-30
8   Ibid.

after death certainly seems to fall in line with Darmani's role in the *Majora's Mask* quest.

Link's next major encounter with an NPC must then be examined in light of these theological implications to validate their wider operation within the game. As previously mentioned, after Goron-Link saves the day in Snowhead, our faithful hero travels to Termina Bay, home of the Zora – a fish-like people who play a recurring role in the Zelda-verse--where he quickly becomes part of another character's story.

In Termina Bay, Link finds Mikau, the guitarist in a Zora band, clinging to life. Link rescues Mikau from a flock of scavenging seagulls and the Zora musician recounts his own tale of failed heroism to Link (in an altogether more entertaining and less serious manner than Darmani). Essentially, the band's lead singer, Lulu, laid some eggs, which were promptly stolen by pirates. Mikau pursued the pirates, but was discovered and attacked. The attack left Mikau at the point of death, but before he goes he tells us, or rather sings to us, that he cannot die in peace as long as the eggs remain away from Lulu, their rightful owner. Mikau, like Darmani, requests Link's aid in the completion of his failed mission. Also like Darmani, Mikau begs Link to heal his soul and, when he passes away, he leaves a mask behind, imbued with his spirit, that allows Link to inhabit his form and achieve the necessary goals. Mikau's soul is healed and we witness him pass into the ether, flanked by Lulu and his bandmates. Just as with Darmani, this moment begins the journey of Mikau's soul towards sanctification.

With Zora-Link, just as Goron-Link before, a shortcoming in life is put right in the spiritual afterlife. Link, after traversing yet another maze-like temple and the many trials it presents, defeats the masked fish that has terrorized the bay, clouded the waters and thrown the Zora community into disarray. With peace restored to the area, much as it was in the Goron Village, it is safe to say that the sanctification of Mikau's spirit is complete. Again, this sanctification occurs in the afterlife and it allows the fulfillment of a shortcoming that heals a character's soul and the restoration of that soul to a healed body.

There is consistency, then, between the two characters that Link helps throughout his adventures in *Majora's Mask*. Both Mikau and Darmani demonstrate that the soul's growth and perfection is not limited to what occurs during life. In fact, both characters count upon this perfection *after* death to offer them peace and release their souls from the spirit-world, or "middle-stage" between full life and full death, and to fulfill the maturation and perfection they sought, but did not achieve, in life. It is worth noting that *Majora's Mask* does not offer us a fully realized picture of Darmani and Mikau's resurrected bodies, reunited with their souls after death in a way consistent with the Christian narrative of restoration.[9] This distinction is vital in that it reveals one key way in which the game does not conform to all aspects of Christian afterlife theology as represented here.

However, the purgatorial theology of *Majora's Mask* does point to a temporal, participatory middle-stage that allows for a type of sanctification resulting in a more perfect state for body and soul. With that established foundation, we can further investigate the theological implications in other aspects of the game's story to answer an earlier question: Why and what is Termina?

Part 2: Link's Sanctification

We have established that the characters within Termina, through their interactions with this world and the next, in many ways suggest a type of purgatorial sanctification. The theological themes we can extract from *Majora's Mask*, however, do not stop with our friends Darmani and Mikau. Link's adventure, apart from his encounters with those two characters, deepens and clarifies the game's reflection of purgatorial theology.

Let's go back to the story's beginning and an initial presupposition about Termina. Link's delirious entry into this alternate

---

9   Again, see 1 Corinthians, Chapter 15 for an extended scriptural statement on death and the resurrected body.

world via a seemingly bottomless black pit indicates entry into the unknown. The hereafter is often described, and even defined, by that very word, "unknown." If we can reasonably assert that Termina is a representation of the afterlife, a familiar yet strange place wrought with fear and containing Majora's Mask, a very present manifestation of evil worn by the Skull Kid, then we must investigate the purpose of this afterlife, if one is to be found, and determine what might be learned from Link's presence there.

First, an important question: What is Link's goal in *Majora's Mask*? As we have established, part of the goal is to restore Termina to safety. Another part is to retrieve Majora's Mask from the Skull Kid and, in so doing, triumph over evil. However, if we look beyond these explicit goals, we see that the goal of improvement of the self (different than self-improvement in that it is not always executed by the one being improved, but potentially by outside forces) becomes a focal point. This is important to our previous discussion of sanctification, because it reiterates the game's apparent view that sanctification may not be complete until a person endures a "significant period of growth and maturation."[10]

Consider these two very notable differences between *Majora's Mask* and almost all of the other *Zelda* titles. First, the primary villain in *Majora's Mask* is not an evil, power-hungry, irredeemable monster like Ganondorf, but simply a lonely kid, driven to folly by his desire to be wanted. Second, consider the message of forgiveness delivered repeatedly throughout the game, most notably by the Ikana King – himself a member of the spirit-world – and, at the game's end, by the ancient giants.

These differences are worth noting because they reorient the game's focus from grand victory over evil forces (though that does occur) or the rescue of a princess to the learning of a timeless lesson, wrought with theological implications that, when applied, serves to improve and indeed purify the life of those who cling to it.

---

10   Jerry L. Walls. "Purgatory for Everyone." *First Things*. 122 (2002): 26-30

During Link's visit to the Stone Temple, he battles the King of Ikana, who, once defeated, delivers one of the most eloquent lines from any game in the *Zelda* series: "Believing in your friends and embracing that belief by forgiving failure… these feelings have vanished from our hearts." The King's sentiment is repeated at the game's end when, after the Skull Kid is tossed aside by the manipulative Majora's Mask, the giants who halt the moon's progress toward Termina ask that the Skull Kid be forgiven.

The giants, who are called guardians throughout *Majora's Mask*, seem, at game's end, to reveal more of their thematic (and, for our purposes, theological) importance. Their power is clear, but what is also clear after Majora is defeated is that these guardians have responded not only because they were asked, but on the condition that both Link and Tatl (his faithful fairy compatriot) forgive the Skull Kid for his misdeeds. Though it is not overtly stated until the final boss has been defeated, the guardian giants - who are, as much as any figures in the game, representations of deity--hint during the game that their hope for and request of Link is this forgiveness rather than physical conquest of the Skull Kid or any other being working against the forces of good. After Gyort, the masked fish, is defeated and the third giant is awakened, he asks, in response to Tatl's plea for the giants' aid, that Link and Tatl "help [their] friend." Tatl takes this to mean that they must awaken the fourth giant in order to halt the moon's imminent collision with Termina. In light of the guardians' later request to "please forgive our friend," and the Skull Kid's subsequent ruminations on being a friend to the giants, it is clear that they have been indicating the Skull Kid as the target of forgiveness.

Part 3: Link Fights the Good Fight, Runs the (Goron) Race and Keeps the Faith

So how does this change in focus from the traditional Zelda format inform our view of Termina and the larger theological implications of *Majora's Mask*? Essentially, if we accept that Termina can be seen as a representation of the afterlife for Link and examine the game's primary concern, that is, moral growth of its main characters rather than sheer physical victory, then it is reasonable to see Link's experience in Termina as another type of purgatorial sanctification, similar in some ways to the perfection of spirit experienced by Darmani and Mikau with Link's help. Link's moral growth, displayed through his greater understanding and practice of forgiveness, seems to come very near the goal of Christian sanctification which, as noted earlier, is the "renewal of humanity in the image of God."[11]

Finally, it is important to note the immense difficulties that Link must go through in order to participate in the sanctification process. The contribution of adversity to sanctification cannot be underestimated; the process is "necessarily painful."[12] This adversity is necessary to Link's growth. In addition, the trials have an effect which is specifically desired by the only figures in *Majora's Mask* that can be considered deified, the guardian giants. Their request of Link to forgive the Skull Kid is the closest instance there is in *Majora's Mask* to divine will. Link has been through the fire and, in the end, he is purified by it, made better through his experience. And though it is true that Link is not, at least to our knowledge, being sanctified to complete righteousness as is the case in the Christian purgatory, he is given the opportunity to take his lesson into life and use it to act more righteously (which logically follows from his experiences).

If all of his trials are capable of providing release from Termina and a level of spiritual growth that contributes to Link's sanctification as not only a hero but a being endowed with the capacity for grace and compassion, then there is little else to consider them but purgatorial. Link does not run from the fire that threatens to devour him. Instead, he

---

11   From the chapter, "Sanctification in the New Testament" H. Ray Dunning. *A Layman's Guide to Sanctification*. Kansas City. Beacon Hill Press, 1991.

12   Jerry L. Walls. "Purgatory for Everyone." *First Things*. 122 (2002): 26-30

suffers the trial so that he might be improved, and so the souls of others might pass peacefully on into the hereafter. It is Link's great privilege that he is able to return to Hyrule from his place in Termina, bringing back with him an understanding of compassion and forgiveness that might be used to lead a more holy life. Like Link, we must actively participate in the honing of our souls toward perfection, not only so that we may pursue God's intention for our lives (and our souls), but that we might, through that pursuit, display the light of God more fully in this world. That, ultimately, is the great theological lesson of *Majora's Mask*: the improvement of the soul's condition towards perfection is as spiritually vital as it is challenging and painful, and we must, through God's grace, strive for it.

On Hylian Virtues: Aristotle, Aquinas and the Hylian Cosmogenesis

Justus Hunter

Imagine you inhabit another world. In this world, trees speak (at least, some of them), fish give gifts and measures of music can teleport. By now, you realize the land I describe is not unlike Hyrule. In fact, if it helps your imagination, you might even say it is Hyrule. Imagine yourself, though, not as a major character in the *Legend of Zelda*, but as an ordinary citizen, a farmer perhaps. Your days are spent planting, harvesting, cooking, etc. – the normal activities of farm life. There is nothing extraordinary about your capabilities, character or genealogy. Now imagine that in some strange turn of events, you find yourself in another realm and stumble upon something unusual: a triangular-shaped, luminescent, levitating object! Naturally, it captures your attention. You are drawn to it. You reach out to touch it and, as you do, in a sudden flash, everything is transformed.

But could you really *stumble upon* the sacred Triforce? Shouldn't some sort of Fate guide the true holder of the Triforce to it? From what we know of the Triforce, though, such a discovery is presumably possible. From the descriptions we have in *A Link to the Past*, the Triforce might be taken up by anyone. It is undirected power, which finds its shape only in union with its possessor. Of course, contingent upon the character of its possessor, a few different possibilities occur. If the possessor has the three virtues of the Triforce (wisdom, courage and power) "in equal balance," he or she receives a wish. However, if the possessor's virtues are in imbalance, then the Triforce splits into its three pieces, the possessor bears whichever piece he or she most characterizes and the other two pieces seek out bearers who exemplify their own virtues. The wish only can be fulfilled by regaining all three pieces and, in the interim, each bearer gains "mystical powers" in their respective virtues.

The latter scenario lies behind *The Legend of Zelda*. Ganon bears the Triforce of Power, Princess Zelda the Triforce of Wisdom and Link the Triforce of Courage. Add a little sexual tension and you have all the necessary elements for suspense and adventure that have made the *Legend of Zelda* a delightful gaming experience for a quarter of a decade.

Let's return to the opening scenario. What might be the world's fate if *you* possessed the Triforce? Let us suppose that you happen to possess power, wisdom and courage "in equal balance." What, then, do you wish for? It would seem to depend a great deal on what amount of these virtues you possess. I suggest that how you define "in equal measure" will make all the difference as to what kind of world Hyrule is.

Suppose I possess power, wisdom and courage in exceptionally meager amounts, nonetheless balanced. What sort of heinous wish might I imagine? Or are we to understand that to say one possesses a measure of virtue, a measure that would satisfy the Triforce's demands, is to say that he would not make a heinous wish? As we see in *A Link to the Past*, the bearer earns whatever wish he possesses in his heart of hearts. For instance, when Ganondorf, Prince of the Thieves, bears the Triforce, his wish is to take over the world. Such is the state of Hyrule, and especially the Sacred/Dark Realm, as we find it in *A Link to the Past*. Not until Link takes possession of the Triforce is the land returned to its original, peaceful state.

In what follows, we will examine what sort of world Hyrule is, in comparison to the world we inhabit as described by Christian theology. Of course, this topic is altogether too complex for a brief essay, so we will consider the comparison in one respect: Virtue. Going forward, we will first observe what the accounts of Hylian cosmogenesis tell us about power, wisdom and courage in Hyrule. Second, I will offer a brief synopsis of two classic accounts of the virtues: (1) Aristotle's, and (2) St. Thomas Aquinas'.[1] Finally, I will make a few comparative

---

1   St. Thomas Aquinas was an Italian Dominican priest who lived from 1225-1274. His most renowned work is the *Summa Theologica* (Summary of Theology, hereafter *ST*), which treats, in four Parts, all major doctrinal teachings of the

observations regarding the Hylian and Thomistic accounts of virtue. The goal of this excursus is both to clarify how Christain theology describes our world and to use that description to clarify the nature of the world of Hyrule.

Hylian Cosmogenesis

According to the Hylian scrolls, the mythical gods descended from a distant nebula to the world and created order and life. The God of Power dyed the mountains red with fire and created land. The God of Wisdom created science and wizardry and brought order to nature. And the God of Courage, through justice and vigor, created life--the animals that crawl the land and the birds that soar in the sky. After the gods had finished their work, they left the world, but not before creating a symbol of their strength, a golden triangle known as the Triforce. A small, but powerful, portion of the essence of the gods was held in this mighty artifact, which was to guide the intelligent life on the world of Hyrule. Although it was an inanimate object, the Triforce had the power to bestow three titles which gave the person who received them great powers: "The Forger of Strength," "The Keeper of Knowledge," and "The Juror of Courage." From its hiding place in the so-called Golden Land where the gods placed it, the Triforce beckoned people from the outside world to seek it in the hope that someone worthy of these titles would find it.

So goes the cosmogenesis (i.e. "beginning of the world") of Hyrule, according to *A Link to the Past*. Even the *Zelda* neophytes, present company included, are aware of the complexities of the Zeldan mythology. Any exploration of the cosmogenesis of Hyrule runs full

---

church. I will use the following translations for Aristotle and Aquinas: Aristotle, *Nicomachean Ethics*, in *The Complete Works of Aristotle: Volume Two*, edited by Jonathon Barnes (Princeton, NJ: Princeton University Press, 1984); Thomas Aquinas, *The "Summa Theologica" of St. Thomas Aquinas*, translated by Fathers of the English Dominican Province, 5 vols. (Notre Dame, IN: Ave Maria Press, 1948).

steam into the characteristically problematic tale developed across decades. The timeline(s) of the multiple *Zelda* games inspires extravagant theories of parallel universes and amorphous temporality. The recklessness and ambiguity of the *Zelda* universe is not only vexing, but accounts for much of the allure. *Zelda's* gaps draw us into the tale, as we inhabit the vantage of the mute protagonist.

Fortunately, Miyamoto & Co. condescended to share more of the Hylian mythology in 1998's *Ocarina of Time*, the first *Zelda* installment on the Nintendo 64 system. The tale is similar to that mentioned above (as are most of the *Zelda* games), yet composed by an ear far more familiar with English:

> Before time began, before spirits and life existed... Three golden goddesses descended upon the chaos that was Hyrule... Din, the goddess of power... Nayru, the goddess of wisdom... Farore, the goddess of courage... Din... With her strong flaming arms, she cultivated the land and created the red earth. Nayru... Poured her wisdom onto the earth and gave the spirit of law to the world. Farore... With her rich soul, produced all life forms who would uphold the law. The three great goddesses, their labors completed, departed for the heavens. And golden sacred triangles remained at the point where the goddesses left the world. Since then, the sacred triangles have become the basis of our world's providence. And, the resting place of the triangles has become the Sacred Realm.[2]

Perhaps the most provocative claim is that the sacred triangles "guide the intelligent life on the world of Hyrule," and, similarly, "have

---

[2] I should note that I will assume something like a unity between these accounts of Creation - not unlike how Jews, Christians, and Muslims read the two creation narratives of Genesis 1-3.

become the basis of our world's providence." The Triforce, an inanimate object, orders and guides the world of Hyrule. Nonetheless, it is not our primary concern here. Rather, we will consider the three goddesses, what they represent, and what their own unique endowment is to the land of Hyrule. To simplify the accounts, I have arranged them into the following chart:

Din	Power	ALttP: dyed the mountains red with fire and created land OoT: cultivated the land and created the red earth	"Forger of Strength"
Nayru	Wisdom	ALttP: created science and wizardry and brought order to nature OoT: gave the spirit of law to the world	"Keeper of Knowledge"
Farore	Courage	ALttP: created life--the animals that crawl the land and the birds that soar in the sky OoT: produced all life forms who would uphold the law	"Juror of Courage"

As noted above, for the sake of comparison, we will refer to these "essences" or "powers" as the Hylian virtues: power, wisdom and courage. Unfortunately, we are given little more information about these virtues. For instance, is this list complete? How are these virtues gained? How are they developed? A brief consideration of two highly developed accounts of virtue will allow us to ponder more deeply the nature of the Hylian virtues. It is to these accounts I now turn.

Aristotelian Virtues

Before I consider a distinctively Christian account of virtue, let's look first at Aristotle's account of virtue. This is helpful for two reasons. First, the primary influences on Thomas Aquinas' account of virtue are Aristotle and Augustine. Second, Aristotle's account gives the context from which we will be comparing Thomas' account and the Hylian account of the virtues, specifically as regards the catalog and nature of the virtues as habitual.

The term "virtue" tends to be used with ambiguity in our culture. For Aristotle, virtue (*aretē*) had a very specific meaning. We will be drawing from the *Nicomachean Ethics* in order to clarify this. Three key terms elucidate the basic structure of Aristotle's understanding of virtue: good (*agathon*), state (*hexis*) and two-fold (*dissos*). Consider the following:

(1) …human *good* turns out to be activity of soul in conformity with virtue,[3] and if there are more than one virtue, in conformity with the best and most complete. (*NE* 1098a15)
(2) If, then, virtues are neither passions nor faculties, all that remains is that they should be *states* (*hexeis*). (*NE* 1106a10)
(3) Virtue, then, is two kinds, intellectual (*dianoētikēs*) and moral (*ēthikēs*); intellectual virtue in the main owes both its birth and its growth to teaching…, while moral virtue comes about as a result of habit (*ēthous*)… (*NE* 1103a14)

One of the concerns of the *Nicomachean Ethics* is to describe

---

3   N.b. I will be translating the term *aretē* as "virtue," but it should be noted that the Barnes translation, cited here, prefers "excellence." I choose virtue, however, not only because the term is more familiar, but also to follow Aquinas's translation of *aretē* as *virtus*.

the human good, the significance of which Aristotle calls "happiness" (*eudaimonia*).[4] For our purposes, the significance of Aristotle's connecting the virtues with the human good is that it locates the conversation in a *teleological* frame. To speak of teleology is to speak of ends, or purposes. So, for example, the end or purpose of a corkscrew is to remove a cork. The end or purpose of medicine is to bring health. The end or purpose of humans, on the other hand, is "happiness." The virtues aim at this purpose. For Aristotle, as an arrow aims at a target, the virtues aim at the human good. Thus, he locates his discussion of human virtues in the context of the ends, goals or purposes of human life. This is the first point to be made: To have virtue is to fulfill the purpose for which human beings exist; to have virtue is to be truly human.

As we see in (2), the virtues are states (*hexeis*). The term rendered state is a participial form of the Greek verb *hexō*, "to have." Quite literally, a state is a "having." This is mirrored by the Latin *habitus*, a participle of the verb *habeo* – again, "to have." So states, or habits, are possessions, things we are "having." Of course, for us to speak of a possession calls to mind something quite different from what Aristotle had in mind. We tend to think of possessions as property. Thus, I *have* the change in my pocket, the coffee in my hand and the Master Sword in my sheath. However, Aristotle has in mind a deeper sense of "having," as we might say someone has health. This deep "having" corresponds to the human good in the following way: "human good turns out to be activity (*energeia*) of soul in conformity with virtue." (*NE* 1098a14) Virtue is a state, a deep "having." The human good is the *activity* of the soul, which has "happiness" as its end. To sum up, virtue is a stable disposition out of which we act toward the good. Out of our courage, we perform courageous acts, which aim at "happiness." Acts, at least the virtuous ones, flow forth from the virtues.

Finally, the virtues are two-fold: intellectual and moral. The

---

4   The designator *human* is important, as it designates what aspect of *the* Good Aristotle is talking about. *The* Good is a larger concept, which includes the human good. The *Nicomachean Ethics* is concerned, primarily, with the human good.

division parallels the division of the soul into the intellectual and appetitive elements.[5] The moral virtues are classified as follows:
1. those concerned with the irrational parts of the soul
    a. courage
    b. temperance
2. those concerned with wealth
    a. liberality
    b. magnificence
3. those concerned with honor
    a. magnanimity
    b. ambition
4. those concerned with others
    a. good temper
    b. (something resembling) friendship
    c. those concerned with speech
        i. truthfulness
        ii. ready-wittedness or tact

---

5   Aristotle (and Aquinas) will talk about three "souls" – intellectual, appetitive, and vegetative. The vegetative soul is concerned with nutrition and growth, and includes all plants and animals. The appetitive soul is concerned primarily with sense perception, and includes all animals (higher and lower). Finally, the intellectual soul is concerned with rationality, and includes the higher animals (humans). See, for instance, "On the Soul."

> d. justice

The intellectual *virtues* are categorized as follows: comprehension, knowledge and philosophical wisdom are excellences of the scientific part, while art and practical wisdom are excellences of the calculative/deliberative part. As we can see, this catalog is much larger than the later, more popular list of (four) cardinal virtues. We will revisit this point later.

Now that we've seen what the virtues are according to Aristotle, consider this brief observation as to how they are acquired. Aristotle contends, "neither by nature, then, nor contrary to nature do virtues arise in us; rather we are adapted by nature to receive them, and are made perfect by habit (*habitus*)." (NE 1103a23) Something arising "by nature," for example, would be natural growth of the human body. There is no habit involved, our bodies just grow. Alternatively, the virtues are not natural, but we are predisposed to develop them. Our development of truthfulness or temperance is possible by repeated, habitual acts corresponding to these virtues. Telling the truth to my wife, son, boss, pastor, parents and the IRS over and over again make me a truthful person. Eventually, it becomes reflexive, or "second nature," to tell the truth. For Aristotle, all the virtues are acquired in this way. While they are made possible naturally, they are acquired by habit.

Thomas' Virtues

As mentioned earlier, Thomas draws primarily from Augustine and Aristotle for his account of the virtues. He accepts Augustine's catalog of the virtues: four cardinal virtues (prudence, courage, temperance, justice) and three theological virtues (faith, hope, love). Augustine's innovation is the addition of the theological virtues to the cardinal virtues, the latter of which he takes from Plato, Cicero and

Ambrose.[6] In accepting Augustine's catalog, and its division between the theological and cardinal virtues, Aquinas also accepts an account of virtue as "infused by God." This will result in tension with Aristotle's account of the virtues as being acquired by human means.

A quick scan through the Treatise on Habits in the *Summa Theologica* I-II reveals the influence of Aristotle on Aquinas. Aquinas begins with a discussion of habit (*habitus*, a parallel construction to Aristotelian *hexis*). He then treats a "special" type of habit, the virtues (*virtutes*). Moreover, his division of the virtues into the moral and intellectual virtues (qq. 57-60) reflects the influence of Aristotle. While the influence of Augustine interjects for a moment to discuss the cardinal virtues, theological virtues and cause of the virtues (God the Creator, qq. 61-63), he returns to Aristotle to discuss the mean of virtue (q. 64), and then works a kind of synthesis between Augustine and Aristotle in discussing the connection of the virtues and their equality (qq. 65-66).[7]

How, though, does Aquinas synthesize these two sources? Jennifer Herdt, in *Putting on Virtue*, explains the synthesis in terms of Aquinas' distinction between infused and acquired virtues.[8] Aristotle, in defining the virtues as "habits," gives an account of the virtues as *acquired*. As I said earlier, for Aristotle the virtues are developed by *human* acts over time--this is all there is.

Augustine disagrees. Augustine, according to Herdt, insists these acquired virtues aim *merely* at the perfection of the human agent (or the common good). Thus, they are not *true* virtue. Their aim is misguided because they aim *merely* at the glory of humanity. For Augustine, true virtue aims at the glory of God. Moreover, it is (and can only be) directly

---

6 Plato includes piety along with the others as a fifth, but it is dropped by Cicero and Ambrose.

7 It should be noted that, in a sense, the entire discussion of the virtues is a work of synthesis, as Aquinas treats Aristotle, Augustine, Scripture and other sources together at almost every point.

8 Jennifer Herdt, *Putting on Virtue: The Legacy of the Splendid Vices* (Chicago: University of Chicago Press, 2008).

given by God - God *infuses* it into the person.

Augustine's legacy regarding the *infused* virtues was propounded by Peter Lombard in the twelfth century, approximately one century before Aquinas. As Herdt observes, "Scholastic theologians after Lombard sought to reconcile the (Aristotelian and Augustinian) approaches to the virtues and commonly did so by distinguishing two distinct kinds of virtues, directed toward different goals."[9] But talk of "different goals" (a human goal and a divine goal) is problematic; it allows for too strong a distinction between the human good and the heavenly good. Correlatively, a "greater separation between earthly flourishing and heavenly flourishing" is rendered.[10]

In light of the aforementioned separation, Aquinas improves upon Lombard by (1) retaining the distinction between *acquired* and *infused* virtues; (2) retaining the distinction between their corresponding ends; and (3) upholding the Augustinian emphasis upon the *ultimate* end (and therefore Good): God. But for Aquinas, God (the ultimate end of human life) orders all other ends. For this reason he calls these other ends "proximate ends."

To sum up, from Aristotle, Aquinas takes an account of *acquired* virtue. From Augustine he takes the ordering effect of the *infused* virtues. However, his judgment of the *acquired* virtues is far more positive than Augustine. Whereas for Augustine the *acquired* virtues are false, Aquinas sees them as aiming at "proximate ends." The *acquired* virtues actually do promote goods (the common good of humanity and individual perfection), just lesser goods that need to be ordered to God, who is the *ultimate* Good.

---

9   Ibid., 75.
10   Ibid., 76.

Hylian Virtues: Redux

Having discussed Thomas, we can make some observations regarding his account and the Hylian account of the virtues. Let's begin by considering Nayru, the second of the Golden Goddesses of Hylian mythology. As we saw in the Hylian cosmogenesis, Nayru brought order by giving law to the world, and the Triforce of Wisdom possesses a portion of her essence. The account is not dissimilar to the Gospel according to John, with its emphasis upon wisdom and the eternal *logos*. In both cases, the creation of the world is done according to an order (*taxis*). In moral theology, this order is developed according to the account of "true" virtue in Augustine, and the directedness of acquired and infused virtue towards proximate and ultimate ends, respectively, in Aquinas. The Hylian cosmogenesis, with its inclusion of order in creation, as well as that order's association with wisdom, *logos* and law, resonates with Aquinas and Augustine. We will return to this point later, in considering whether or not the Hylian virtues are natural, acquired or infused.

It is always precarious to argue from silence, so we will attempt to focus upon what is said in the Hylian cosmogenesis and mythology in contrasting the various catalogs of virtue. However, it should be noted that this limitation to three is significantly shortened from the longer catalogs of Aristotle, Augustine and Aquinas. Of course, this might be easily dismissed by suggesting there may be a larger catalog than we know from the Hylian cosmogenesis.

That being said, the most obvious difference between what we have dubbed the Hylian virtues and Thomas' virtues is the presence of the virtue of power in the Hylian catalog. The correlation between Hylian courage and Thomas' fortitude, as well as Hylian wisdom and Thomas' prudence, is clear enough. One might quip that the issue with power is one of translation, but it remains to be seen how easily a conversion might be made from *power* to either *justice* or *temperance*. Aristotle's catalog may find resonance under the category of virtues associated with honor (to wit, magnanimity and ambition), but as it turns out, these virtues are the very ones which come under attack by both Augustine and Aquinas. Moreover, the attribution of the virtue of power to Ganon reveals its potentially diabolical nature (for instance, his evil wishes render the Sacred World darkened in *A Link to the Past*). Certainly, the virtue of power is problematic when considered from the vantage of Christian theology.

To press a bit deeper, beyond the catalogs, there are at least three points worthy of reflection in comparing the Thomistic and Hylian accounts of virtue: (1) the connection of the virtues; (2) the nature of the virtues as natural, acquired or infused; and (3) the source of the virtues.

To begin, the virtues, for Aquinas, are intimately connected. At *ST* I-II, q. 65, a.1 he appeals to the Gospel of Luke, Augustine, Gregory, Aristotle and Cicero in arguing the moral virtues (i.e. cardinal virtues) are connected with one another. His point is that for a moral virtue to be perfect (say wisdom, for instance), it must be accompanied by the other virtues (such that the truly wise person will also be temperate, courageous, just, etc.).

We find a similarity in the Hylian virtues. According to *Ocarina of Time*, only those who possess power, wisdom and courage "in equal balance" will be able to possess the entirety of the Triforce without its splintering. As mentioned earlier, how you define the phrase "in equal measure," will make all the difference as to what kind of world Hyrule is. The Hylian virtues (when perfect) are connected (as in Aquinas' account); the only possibility for possession of the Triforce without its splintering is in the hands of one with an equal measure of power, wisdom and courage. An ultimately diabolical wish, the sort Ganon might make, would be rendered impossible. Of course, the possibility of a regathering is possible, which is the very task we find Ganon in process of in several installments of the *Legend of Zelda*. Nonetheless, it would seem Hyrule protects against this possibility as well by the provision of the "Hero of Time."

It is also unclear whether and to what extent Hylian virtues are natural, acquired or infused. We have a sense that all three cases exist. For instance, Princess Zelda is apparently infused with wisdom and magical powers, such that the Triforce of Wisdom naturally seeks her out. Ganon, on the other hand, seems to habitually develop his power as the Prince of Thieves. His bloody victory grants him the right to the Triforce and reign over the Sacred Realm in *A Link to the Past*. In Link, we seem to have both a natural courage, as well as its development over the course of time.

  Finally, the source of the virtues is distinct in each account. According to Thomas, the virtues are caused by God in one of two ways. First, while Thomas will distinguish between the moral virtues acquired by habituation and the theological virtues infused by God, the moral virtues are nonetheless caused by God. The *Summa Theologica* opens with an excursus on God, first, in terms of essence, but immediately (and integrally) followed by an account of God as Creator. This is the paradigm through which Aquinas always thinks of God and humanity: God as Creator and humanity as creaturely. Thus, even the *acquired* virtues are a gift, caused by God. They are not, however, given *immediately*. The infused virtues are caused immediately by God (*immediate a Deo causari*, q. 63, a. 4). This immediacy distinguishes the infused virtues in their lack of a mediation (say, for instance, by nature). We might say, they are *directly* given by God, whereas the acquired virtues are *indirectly* given, resting upon the activity of the human agent as they do.

  On the other hand, in the land of Hyrule, the source of the virtues is unclear. Apparently, they correspond to the Golden Goddesses in some way, as the "essences" of the Goddesses which imbue the bearers of pieces of the Triforce with mystical powers. Do the virtues come from these absent Creators? Or are they given and ordered by the inanimate Triforce? Moreover, we have seen the "mixed" nature of the Hylian virtues; they are sometimes natural, sometimes acquired and sometimes infused. In the final analysis, this is perhaps the most consistent thread we find with the Hylian virtues; our account is incomplete. Our consideration of Aristotle and Aquinas has helped a great deal in articulating the puzzles and gaps we get from the *Legend of Zelda* regarding the order of its world and the virtues contained therein. Moving forward, we must watch and wait, as the *Legend of Zelda* unfolds, to understand and imagine what sort of world it is we inhabit when we're embodied by the mute and green-tuniced "Hero of Time."

Perhaps the answers await us in future releases, but more often than not, I suspect we will find more questions. However, we've seen that the process of seeking to articulate an account of the Hylian virtues enables us to better understand not only the world of Hyrule, but our own world as well. We begin to see the profound difference living in a created world, ordered according to Christ (as Paul says in Colossians 1) and infused with the grace of God, makes for us.

We do not live in Hyrule. Trees do not converse with us. Fish do not give us presents. Measures of music cannot teleport us across town. Our world has no levitating Triforce. However, as Thomas contends, what we have is a graced creation and a gracious Creator. One of these graces are the virtues, and for these we can be grateful.

High Rule? Vintage Virtue in The Legend of Zelda

Benjamin B. DeVan

In honor of Matthew, Gray and Laurie Brannan for their friendship, hospitality and for introducing me to The Legend of Zelda.

As with other beginnings (like Genesis 1), *The Legend of Zelda* opens with chaos and darkness over the land, the waters and the surface of the deep.[1] The Prince of Darkness, Ganon, and his minions have overrun the peaceful kingdom of Hyrule, stolen the mystical Triforce of Power, kidnapped princess Zelda and set their eyes on a second Triforce that Zelda stewarded, the Triforce of Wisdom.

Anticipating Ganon's move to seize the Triforce of Wisdom, Zelda divided and scattered it into eight parts, carefully spiriting each part to a different hideaway in Hyrule. Zelda charged Impa, her nursemaid, to find a champion with sufficient courage to reassemble the Triforce of Wisdom and challenge Ganon's reign of terror. Like the people of Fantasia in *The Neverending Story* encountering Atreyu, Gandalf finding Bilbo, Frodo and Sam in *The Hobbit* and *The Lord of the Rings*, or Saul entertaining the Biblical David's offer to face Goliath, providence would lead Impa to the unlikeliest of persons.[2]

---

[1] Cf. Genesis 1; *The Legend of Zelda* Instruction Manual (Nintendo / Capcom, 1986), pp. 3-4.

[2] See 1 Samuel 17; Michael Ende, *The Neverending Story* (trans. Ralph Manheim, Stuttgart, 1979, NY: Doubleday, 1983) where the realm is "Fantastica" or "Phantasien," *The NeverEnding Story* (Neue Constantin Film, Bavaria Studios, Westdeutscher Rundfunk [WDR], Warner Bros. Pictures, Producers Sales Organization, April 6, 1984, West Germany); *The Lord of the Rings* (New Line Cinema, WingNut Films, The Saul Zaentz Company, 2001-2003, USA); J.R.R. Tolkien, *The Hobbit: There and Back Again* (UK: George Allen & Unwin Ltd., 1937); J.R.R. Tolkien, *The Lord of the Rings: 50th Anniversary Edition* (1954, NY: Houghton Mifflin, 2004).

Exhausted from fleeing Ganon's goons, Impa found herself surrounded and seemingly out of options when a youthful journeyman appeared. He deftly parried Ganon's henchman like another youthful journeyman, Moses, who once defended Zipporah and her sisters.[3] Could this "young lad," Link, be the champion Impa sought?

Pouring her heart out, Impa regaled Ganon's cruelties to Link, pleading on behalf of Hyrule and Princess Zelda. Burning with a sense of justice, Link resolved to reunite the scattered Triforce of Wisdom to help sustain him in facing Ganon, rescuing Princess Zelda, and restoring peace to Hyrule.

Another Young Lad:

Like Link, I was a "young lad" when I first discovered *The Legend of Zelda* flashing on my friend Matthew's television screen with a tangled knot of cords trailing to and from a freshly assembled, newly minted *Nintendo Entertainment System (NES)*. It would be half a year or more until I obtained my own *NES* and *Zelda* game, the latter thanks to my dad's resourcefulness in finding a rare, used game cartridge when local stores ran out of stock.

Fortunately for me, Matthew and his parents were indulgent and hospitable enough to allow me the chance to gradually reassemble the Triforce of Wisdom and defy Ganon with Link as my medium.

If you had asked me at the time how I thought *The Legend of Zelda* illustrated or informed ethics or Christian theology, I might have (had I known well enough) spoken like a pre-teen Tertullian, "What hath Nintendo to do with Jesus? What hath Hyrule to do with 'rules' or with Heaven?"[4] But since for me, playing Nintendo was like a taste of heaven, I probably would have just shrugged politely and returned to the joy of

---

3   Exodus 2:15-21. All Biblical quotes from the New International Version (2010 edition, CO: Biblica Incorporated) unless otherwise noted. Cf. *The Legend of Zelda* Instruction Manual, p. 4.
4   Cf. Tertullian, De Praescriptione Haereticorum, Chapter 7.

the game as quickly as possible.

Twenty years later, aspiring to earn my bread and butter as an ethicist and comparative religions professor, I have a few more thoughts on the matter. What hath ethics to do with Hyrule? Are there illustrations or parallels between *The Legend of Zelda* and Christian theology? I think there are. We will look at two vintage games specifically, *The Legend of Zelda* and *Zelda II: The Adventure of Link*. Since we've already heard the backstory for *The Legend of Zelda*, let's review *The Adventure of Link* as well.

Zelda II: The Adventure of Link commences at an unspecified time after *The Legend of Zelda* when Link is a strapping sixteen year old. Like so many fictional females of folktale lore, Zelda is under a sleeping spell.[5] Ganon's minions are regrouping and hoping to resurrect Ganon by killing Link and ritually sprinkling Link's blood over Ganon's ashes.[6] To awaken Zelda, Link must employ not "True Love's Kiss," but the restorative synergy of the Triforce of Power, the Triforce of Wisdom and a third Triforce of Courage concealed within the "Great Palace." It is here that Link must confront his shadow (Dark Link) in the Valley of Death (in contrast with "Death Mountain" in *The Legend of Zelda*, cf. Psalm 23).[7] To access the Great Palace, Link quests to return the shards of a magic crystal to six lesser (not so great?) palaces, overcome fierce enemies and help Hyrule villagers along the way.[8]

---

5   For attentive gamers, there is ambivalence about whether this is the same Princess Zelda from *The Legend of Zelda* or her ancient namesake preserved agelessly by the sleeping spell. Cf. http://www.nintendo.com/wii/online/virtual-console/games/detail/f59_izTMLrgCYNvtvbKZSErv-sYsSKX0; http://zelda.com/universe/game/link/; *Zelda II: The Adventure of Link* Instruction Manual (Japan: Nintendo, 1987). All websites accessed January 27, 2011, unless otherwise noted.

6   "Gibdos" are also hungry for Link's blood in *The Legend of Zelda*, cf. http://zelda.com/universe/pedia/g.jsp.

7   "True Love's Kiss" is a song from Enchanted in homage to Disney classics like *Snow White and the Seven Dwarfs*. See Michael Buckley, "Menken & Schwartz Are 'Enchanted;' Plus Bosco, Chenoweth, 'Hairspray,'" *Playbill* (November 18, 2007), http://www.playbill.com/news/article/113379.html.

8   The encyclopedia at the official "Zelda Universe" site, http://www.

Turning to ethics and theology, there are at least three sets of "high rules" in Link's first two adventures ripe for reflection. First, we will look beyond *The Legend of Zelda* and poke at a brief theological ethics of gaming in general. Next, we will dive back into Hyrule, ask how Link and his encounters parallel and illustrate aspects of integrity, reciprocal (as well as Christ-like) altruism, Christian doctrine and "just war" or justifiable (non) violence. Finally, we will inquire into the implicit foundation for Link's morality and why that foundation matters.

Virtue and Virtual Play

Is playing video games ethical? If you haven't had the following conversation with a friend, critic or authority figure, prepare yourself. "Gaming (as Blind Melon crooned in the nineties about reading) fritters or 'rips' your life away!"[9] "What a waste of time and energy!" "Good for nothing but eye-hand coordination!" "Virtual and gaming relationships aren't 'real' relationships. Get a life!"

These indignant barbs ignore positive features of gaming, like collaboration; camaraderie (especially in multi-player games); problem-solving; building cognitive skills; simulating risky real-life situations; sporadic "great escapes;" Sabbath-like rest and relaxation.

But the critics and naysayers have a point. Anyone who saw *South Park*'s Emmy-award winning, "Make Love, Not Warcraft," based on the "massive multi-player" (not just multi-player!) online game *World of Warcraft*, may cringe with recognition at the overindulgent fixations by Eric, Kenny, Kyle, Stan and other characters whose lives and health

---

zelda.com/universe/pedia/ in the entry, "Magic Crystal," indicates *returning* crystal shards to different palaces in contrast with other entries on spells and palace guardians which talk about Link *recovering* the shards of the crystal and using them with or instead of the three Triforces to awaken Zelda. The visuals and narrative of the game itself favor the "Magic Crystal" entry.
9   Blind Melon, "No Rain," Blind Melon (Capital Records, September 22, 1992).

deteriorate as they become gross and engrossed, virtually inseparable from the game.[10]

As William David Spencer explores in "Cyber Marriage, Virtual Adultery, Real Consequences, and the Need for a Techno-Sexual Ethic," gaming enthusiasts and other technoids can spasmodically blend virtual and non-virtual worlds in ways that not only fail to be fruitful, but plummet toward disaster.[11] Compulsive gamers prudently pre-empt this type of mania by (re)visiting Aldous Huxley's, *Brave New World*, or movies like *Inception*, *The Matrix* or *Repo Men*, where virtual dream worlds become the only "realities" some characters seem capable of experiencing.[12] Unbridled technophilia, to modify Marx, is the sigh of the obsessed creature and an opiate for the masses.[13]

On the other hand, gaming can provide catharsis and a chance (as with sports, though not always with the same physical benefits) to blow off steam, harmlessly channel competitive spirits and function as a training ground for careful decision making. Gamers can (re)enact morality plays, improvising as games allow in ways redolent of ancient peoples retelling myths and performing rituals, recreating and participating in cosmic or epic dramas.[14]

---

10   South Park, Episode 147 "Make Love, Not Warcraft" (Comedy Central, October 4, 2006). Cf. Gollum's obsession with the "One Ring" in *Lord of the Rings*, and *South Park*'s parody of that obsession in Episode 92, "The Return of the Fellowship of the Ring to the Two Towers" (Comedy Central, November 13, 2002).

11   William David Spencer, "Cyber Marriage, Virtual Adultery, Real Consequences, and the Need for a Techno-Sexual Ethic," *Africanus Journal* 2:2 (November, 2010), pp. 14-22.

12   Aldous Huxley, Brave New World (NY: Harper & Bros., 1932) and Brave *New World Revisited* (NY: Harper & Bros., 1958); *Inception* (Warner Bros., July 8, 2010, UK); *The Matrix* (Warner Bros., March 31, 1999, USA); *Repo Men* (Universal Pictures, March 19, 2010, USA).

13   Karl Marx, Contribution to the Critique of Hegel's Philosophy of Right (1843, reprinted in Karl Marx, *Early Writings*, NY: Penguin, 1975, 1992), p. ccxxxix.

14   For a contemporary brief and accessible overview of classic perspectives on ritual and myth among primordial and modern people, see Bruce Sheiman, "Religion is Finding Life's Meaning: Myth, Ritual, and the Sacred" in *An*

As one contemporary ritual and myth-making medium, gaming incarnates and is subject to what G.K. Chesterton called, "The Ethics of Elfland," via the macrocosmic universes games mirror or create, and the simulated microscopic scenarios embedded within the narratives of each game. Chesterton wrote that his earliest and most enduring ethical training came from fairy tales told to him in nursery. For example, the lesson of *Cinderella* was the same as "the Magnificat—*exaltavit humiles*." The premise of *Beauty and the Beast* is, "a thing must be loved *before* it is loveable." The fearsome allegory *Sleeping Beauty* "tells us how the human creature was blessed with all birthday gifts, yet cursed with death; and how death also may perhaps be softened to a sleep."[15]

A century after Chesterton, gaming often stands in for or with fairy tales and other mythic stories to nurture a sense of awe and wonder, right and wrong through larger than life villains, superhuman heroes and role models. For adults, gaming further complements or substitutes curling up with a good book or popping brain candy from a favorite movie or show at day's end.

As playfully enacted myths, games can be what C.S. Lewis called "good dreams," whose noblest elements prefigure and provoke longing for the ultimate reality fulfilled by God in Jesus Christ.[16] Anticipating bemused atheists who might interpret Lewis's appeal to myth as "magical thinking" in a delusional rather than an imaginative sense, Lewis and fellow professor and fantasist J.R.R. Tolkien conceived of Christianity as "myth become fact."

In the life of Jesus, "the old myth of the Dying God,
without ceasing to be myth (or losing its mythic themes),

Atheist Defends Religion: Why Humanity Is Better Off with Religion than without It (NY: Penguin, 2009), pp. 1-22.
15   G.K. Chesterton, Orthodoxy (NY: John Lane Company, 1909), pp. 89-89, digitized at www.books.google.com.
16   C.S. Lewis, Mere Christianity (NY: HarperSanFrancisco, 1952, 2001), p. 50.

comes down from the heaven of legend and imagination to the earth of history and reality. It *happens*—at a particular date, in a particular place, followed by definable historical consequences."[17]

Tolkien and Lewis's feminist friend and fellow scholar, the playwright and mystery writer Dorothy L. Sayers, reiterates in her essay, "The Greatest Drama Ever Staged," that pagan yarns such as Aeschylus' *The Eumenides* contain stories about reconciling humans and the divine through divine or redemptive suffering, but "in most theologies, the god is supposed to have suffered and died in some remote and mythical period of prehistory. The Christian story, on the other hand, starts off briskly in St. Matthew's account with a place and a date."[18]

Lewis also offers a solidly Christian approach to defining and evaluating *Miracles*,[19] and turns the "wishful thinking" charge back on

---

[17] C.S. Lewis, "Myth Become Fact," in God in the Dock: Essays on Theology *and Ethics* (ed. Walter Hooper) in *The Collected Works of C.S. Lewis: Three Bestselling Works Complete in One Volume* (NY: Inspirational Press, 1970, 1996), p. 343. Cf. Colin Duriez, *Tolkien and C.S. Lewis: The Gift of Friendship* (NJ: Hidden Spring, 2003); C.S. Lewis, "Religion: Reality or Substitute?" in *Christian Reflections* (ed. Walter Hooper) in *The Collected Works of C.S. Lewis*, pp. 199-202; C.S. Lewis, "Checkmate" in *Surprised by Joy: The Shape of My Early Life* (NY: Harcourt, Brace & Company,1955), pp. 205-221; J.R.R. Tolkien, *Tolkien On Fairy Stories* (Verlyn Flieger and Douglas A. Anderson, eds., NY: HarperCollins, 2008).

[18] Dorothy L. Sayers, "The Greatest Drama Ever Staged" (1938, reprinted in *Letters to a Diminished Church: Passionate Arguments for the Relevance of Christian Doctrine*, TN: W Publishing Group, 2004), p. 3.

[19] C.S. Lewis, Miracles: A Preliminary Study (1947, revised 1960, restored 1996, NY: HarperCollins, 2001); Lewis, "Miracles" and "The Grand Miracle," in *The Collected Works*, pp. 313-321, 354-359. Cf. Francis S. Collins, *The Language of God: A Scientist Presents Evidence for Belief* (NY: Free Press, 2006), pp. 33, 44, 47-54; Thomas Crean, "Professor Dawkins and Miracles" in *God is No Delusion* (UK: Family Publications, 2007), pp. 50-61; R. Douglas Geivett, "Why I Believe in the Possibility of Miracles" and Gary R. Habermas, "Why I Believe the Miracles of Jesus Actually Happened" in Paul K. Hoffman and Norman L. Geisler (eds.), *Why I Am a Christian: Leading Thinkers Explain Why They Believe* (MI: Baker Books

Freud by posing that atheists may be motivated by wishfully thinking that there is no transcendent accountability or authority. Maybe the near universal longing for God is not neurosis. "If I find in myself a desire which no other experience in this world can satisfy, the most probable explanation is that I was made for another world."[20]

As with other imperfect vehicles of joy, truth and beauty, gaming at its best stokes desire for New Creation by momentarily and simultaneously slaking and whetting our thirst for "living water" (John 4) and our hunger for "the bread of life" (John 6), creatively anticipating what "No eye has seen, no ear has heard, no mind has conceived what God has prepared for those who love him" (1 Corinthians 2:9).[21] All such goodness, truth and beauty rightly perceived evoke mindfulness and point to the Source and Fountain for all goodness, truth and beauty.

Vintage Virtue in Hyrule:

In this section we will examine various versions of altruism and their interplay with other ethics and theologies in Hyrule. Altruism is a key ethic embedded in the first two *Zelda* installments. Widely defined as the opposite of selfishness, altruism often is characterized as doing good for others without guarantee of immediate or obvious personal benefit in return.

Philosophers, theologians and other thinkers have puzzled over what motivates seemingly selfless behavior, sometimes denying outright that pure altruism exists. They suggest that what appears to be altruism must be driven by hidden, ulterior or unconscious motives like building

---

2001, Revised and Expanded 2006), pp. 105-119, 120-134; Colin Humphreys, *The Miracles of Exodus: A Scientist's Discovery of the Extraordinary Natural Causes of the Bible Stories* (NY: HarperCollins, 2003).

20   Lewis, Mere Christianity, pp. 136-137; "Bulverism" in The Collected Works pp. 484-488. Cf. C. Stephen Evans, *Why Believe: Reason and Mystery as Pointers to God* (1986, MI: William B. Eerdmans, Revised 1996), p. 57.

21   For "living water" imagery, see Jeremiah 2:13, 17:13; Zechariah 14:18; John 4:10-11, 7:38; Revelation 7:17.

a reputation, sexual or social attractiveness associated with generosity, hope for future payback (including, "treasures in heaven where moth and rust do not destroy," Matthew 6:19-21) and the possibility that recipients of one's beneficence will return the kindness later. "One good turn deserves another." Or, to adapt another aphorism, "I'll scratch your back now, if you scratch mine later." At worst, this recalls the mafia don, "I'll do you a favor, you'll do me a favor, or you'll sleep with the fishes."[22]

But this "reciprocal" form of altruism in doing good to others who may or may not do good to you in return need not be classified as cynical or sinister. One can admit that mixed or multiple motives are in play while benefiting from and encouraging such altruism. In fact, *The Legend of Zelda* and *Zelda II: The Adventure of Link* reinforce reciprocal altruism.

In both games, it's unclear to what degree villagers, merchants and others in Hyrule are aware of Link's quest. Some beg Link, "Please save our town!" "You must save Hyrule!" Others help Link without immediately receiving anything tangible in return, while still others require networking (e.g. "Only townsfolk may cross this river!" "I am much too busy to talk to a stranger," the note from Bagu to the river man in *The Adventure of Link*, and the "Letter to the Old Woman" in *The Legend of Zelda*). They want evidence of strength and goodwill before they assist, cooperate or trade with Link (e.g. "Come back when you are ready." "Do you have the seven magic containers?")

Among Hyrulians, there are also faux friends/villagers. Like wolves in sheep's clothing (cf. Matthew 7:15-16, 2 Corinthians 11:13-15), "eyes of Ganon" actively work to cripple Link. Apparently renegade wizards/old men in *The Legend of Zelda*'s Second Quest insist, "Leave

---

[22] Cf. The Godfather (Alfran Productions, Paramount Pictures, March 15, 1972, USA).

your money or your life!"[23] The wise Link, if he has sufficient cash, parts with the coin. As Jesus propounded, "What good is it to gain the whole world, yet lose or forfeit your life/self/soul?"[24] In contrast, the Goriya of Tantari in *The Adventure of Link* steals the Ruto town trophy and effectively gives up his or her life/soul for a trinket. Like Gollum in *The Hobbit*, the Goriya perpetually skulks in a cave north of Ruto, consumed by her (or his) stolen "precious."

Still, the general trend for human and human-like Hyrulians, despite all of this, is altruism. Elderly women, young women and magical fairies heal Link's infirmities or refill his magic containers. The first old man/wizard that Link meets in *The Legend of Zelda* gives Link a sword, telling him, "It's dangerous to go alone, take this!" In both games, wizards or wise/old men teach magic, give heart containers, swords, "water of life" and (perhaps more profitably than altruistically) sell bomb pouches to Link. Moblin turncoats betray Ganon by stocking Link with extra rupees (coin), while a non-aggressive bat and bit (or bot) offer information in *The Adventure of Link*, blurring lines between "enemy races" and friends.

In other instances, it is Link who takes the initiative. Link defends Impa, quests to save Zelda and Hyrule, returns lost mirrors and town trophies, shares "water of life" with the ill, rescues kidnapped children or captured fairies and gives a cup of cold water (cf. Matthew 10:42 and Proverbs 25:25) to a thirsty villager. Reinforcing the principle of reciprocal altruism, Link is repeatedly rewarded for acts of kindness with assorted apprenticeships, e.g. new sword moves (learned from sword masters), new magic, relevant information and other tools to assist him in his quest.

---

23 Do the wizards/old men like Gandalf/Mithrandir in Lord of the Rings mirror spirit beings, angels and demons? Cf. J.R.R. Tolkien, *The Letters of J.R.R. Tolkien* (Selected and edited by Humphrey Carpenter with the assistance of Christopher Tolkien, Boston, MA: George Allen & Unwin, 1981), pp. 202-207, 354, 410-411.
24 Cf. Matthew 16:26; Mark 8:46; Luke 9:25.

Since Christianity teaches a "fallen" or partially depraved humanity, Christians need not be stymied by assertions that altruism can have mixed or multiple motives. This remains true even as we seek to purify our motives in Christ-likeness, inviting the Holy Spirit to sanctify and equip us in pursuing righteousness for its own sake and for the benefits it bestows on us, on the people we interact with and, by extension, on all facets of creation that God entrusts us to steward.

As we have seen already, Jesus motivated his disciples partly by appealing to heavenly reward or "delayed gratification," as psychologists would say, or a sound eternal investment with potentially infinite, rather than temporary, dividends from an economics perspective. To put it another way: "What we do in life echoes in eternity."[25] C.S. Lewis clarifies:

> (A negative) idea of unselfishness carries with it not primarily securing of good things for others, but of going without them ourselves, as if our abstinence and not their happiness was the important point…The New Testament has lots to say about self-denial, but not… as an end in itself…The notion that to desire our own good and earnestly to hope for the enjoyment of it is a bad thing…has crept in from Kant and the Stoics and is no part of the Christian faith…(If we consider) the staggering nature of the rewards promised in the Gospels, it would seem that Our Lord finds our desires not too strong, but too weak. We are half-hearted creatures fooling about with drink and sex and ambition when infinite joy is offered us, like an ignorant child who wants to go on making mud pies in a slum because he cannot imagine what is meant by the offer of a holiday at the sea.[26]

---

25   Maximus in Gladiator (Dreamworks SKG, Universal Pictures, Scott Free Productions, Red Wagon Entertainment, May 1, 2000 USA).
26   C.S. Lewis, "The Weight of Glory," in The Weight of Glory and Other

Lewis deftly anticipates the objection that this makes Christianity a "mercenary affair" by differentiating between varieties of reward for altruistic behavior. One variety of behavior has no natural connection with its reward. Philosophers might call this a "second order" good. The other is the "activity itself in consummation," a "first order" good.[27] For example, if a man marries a woman for her money, the marriage is a "second order good," a means to an end. But if he marries her for love, marital joy is the "activity itself in consummation" (in more ways than one!). Thus, altruism may thus be doubly motivated by desire for one's own good and for the good of other people. When Link, Zelda and the people of Hyrule interact altruistically, they nurture reciprocity, relationship and synergy that otherwise would not have been possible.

Yet at a subtle level, Link embodies more than "reciprocal" altruism by acting with a spirit of justice, defending the weak and risking his life for Zelda and Hyrule. "Greater love has no one than this, to lay down one's life for one's friends" (John 15:13).[28] Is Link then a Christ figure? There are hints that Jesus serves as partial inspiration for Link's character. For example: Ganon's minions believe Link's blood contains the power of resurrection. Link walks on water like Jesus, though Link requires the winged boots. Link's shields and gravestones in both games bear the cross (though Link's shield in later games bears the sign of the Triforce.) *The Adventure of Link* once references a church bell ringing. Link descends beneath Death Mountain in one game and Death Valley in the other to defeat the Prince of Darkness and confront the Shadow/

Ad*dresses* (1949, NY: Simon & Schuster, 1996), pp. 25-26.
27   Lewis, "The Weight of Glory," pp. 26-27.
28   Cf. One among several possible endings for the NES game *Castlevania II: Simon's Quest* (Konami, April 28, 1987), is where Simon Belmont succumbs to his wounds, laying down his life (or shedding his blood) for Castlevania, but not in the way Simon's bloodthirsty nemesis Dracula expects. See also *Ninja Gaiden* (Tecmo, December 1988), where Ryu risks his life for his father, and Ryu's father gives his life to save Ryu.

Dark/False Link.[29] However, even if Jesus is not an inspiration for Link, he surely qualifies as one of the "good dreams" styled by Lewis, Sayers and Tolkien. Link is "humble to the end...a symbol of courage, strength and wisdom...tales of his bravery will never cease, and his legend will never ever die."[30]

It should be noted that Link resembles, in some ways, not only Jesus but "heroes of old, men of renown" (Genesis 6:4) and Hindu figures like Lord Rama. Thus, one does not find exclusively Christian parallels and imagery in the first two *Legend of Zelda* installments, or in the backstories for later games in the series.[31] The mode of the game "resetting" when Link dies in course of play, with him retaining much of the game player's history resonates with Hindu and Buddhist views of reincarnation where merit or demerit from past lives accumulates in the present incarnation, though this element of Link's existence likely results from qualities inherent to the medium of the video game rather than to artistic choice. There is also a "second chance" to do things right, like the re-weavings of the pattern in Robert Jordan's *Wheel of Time* or, of course,

---

29   Link must also figuratively "descend into death" in The Legend of Zelda to receive the strongest "Magical Sword" from the wizard/old man in the graveyard via a hidden stairway in an (empty?) tomb. Death and resurrection are similarly insinuated as "Deep Magic from the Dawn of Time" and "Deeper Magic from Before the Dawn of Time" in C.S. Lewis, *The Lion, the Witch and the Wardrobe* (1950, NY: HarperCollins, no date), e.g. pp. 147, 171.

30   Cf. Jesus, "Heaven and earth will pass away, but my words will never pass away" (Matthew 24:35; Mark 13:31; Luke 21:33); "Link," http://www.zelda.com/universe/pedia/l.jsp; Isaiah 9:6 traditionally refers to Messiah as "Prince of Peace," while *The Legend of Zelda* proclaims after Link rescues Zelda, "Finally, peace returns to Hyrule." Jesus is revealed as the Divine "Logos" or embodied wisdom in the Gospel of John, e.g. Ben Witherington, "Wisdom in Person: Jesus the Sage," in *Jesus the Sage: The Pilgrimage of Wisdom* (MN: Augsburg Fortress, 1994), pp. 147-208.

31   Cf. e.g. R.K. Narayan, The Ramayana: A Shortened Modern Prose Version of *the Indian Epic (Penguin Classics)* (NY: Penguin, 1972, 2006); the "Triforce" as created by "goddesses" at http://www.zelda.com/universe/pedia/t.jsp.

God reestablishing spiritual life and vitality even after multiple falls into sin or temptation. Quoting Lewis again:

> (As to) chronic temptations...*No amount* of falls will really undo us if we keep picking ourselves up (or allow God to pick us up) each time. We shall...be very muddy and tattered children by the time we reach home. But the bathrooms are all ready, the towels put out, and the clean clothes in the airing cupboard. The only fatal thing is to lose one's temper and give it up. It is when we notice the dirt that God is most present in us: it is the very sign of His presence.[32]

Unlike some "heroes of old," Link, like Jesus and R.K. Narayan's portrayal of Rama, is "humble" and embodies "Just War" by limiting violence exclusively to violently vicious enemy aggressors.[33] Link cannot and will not cheat or attack merchants and others, though he certainly has the opportunity and ability.

Link is bound presumably by his integrity not to overpower or take other people's goods by force, even for use in his noble cause. Link even refrains from attacking old men/wizards who demand money or a heart container, nor will he wrangle with those who stipulate (when Link burns or bombs a door unbidden), "Pay me the door repair charge." Nor will Link slay the hungry goriya who opposes him with non-lethal force (non-lethal, unless Link stupidly hangs around to be barraged by the nearby fireballs) in *The Legend of Zelda* level seven.

There's no denying, though, Link is not a pacifist. Sword

---

32   C.S. Lewis, Letters (20 January, 1942) in The Business of Heaven: Daily *Readings from C.S. Lewis* (ed. Walter Hooper, FL: Harcourt, 1984) p. 17, italics in original. Cf. Robert Jordan and Brandon Sanderson, *The Gathering Storm: Book Twelve of the Wheel of Time* (NY: Tor, 2009), p. 759.
33   Cf. J. Daryl Charles, Between Pacifism and Jihad: Just War and Christian *Tradition* (IL: InterVarsity Press, 2005); Walter Wink, *The Powers That Be: Theology for a New Millennium* (NY: Doubleday, 1998).

fighting is a central component in each *Legend of Zelda* game. In the end, it takes bloodshed to bring Ganon to justice, even though Link does not begin his meeting with Ganon by fighting, but by holding aloft the Triforce of Wisdom. Rather than standing down, Ganon fires a first strike. Link's "sense of justice" will not permit Ganon to wage tyranny indefinitely, or to see injustice continue ad infinitum if he can end it. As Martin Luther King, Jr. observed, "Peace is not the absence of conflict but the presence of justice."[34] AMEN!

The Source for Link's Morality and Why It Matters:

What or who is the immediate source for morality in Hyrule and why does this matter? The immediate source is the game *creator*, the game *designer*(s). Does this have implications for a source of morality beyond Hyrule's digital shores? I believe it does.

The creative design of the gaming universe(s) inhabited by Link, Zelda and other Hyrule citizens parallels God's work as the Grand Designer, High Rule(r) and Ultimate Source for morality in our world, whether or not people directly acknowledge it.[35] The Triune God Christians worship does not arbitrarily pronounce some motives, thoughts and actions as evil and others as good. He is, rather, a God whose very nature is totally and fundamentally Beauty, Goodness and Truth itself.[36] The second person of the Divine Trinity, who becomes incarnate as Jesus, is the true and better "Link" between human and

---

[34] In Coretta Scott King, The Words of Martin Luther King, Jr. (NY: Newmarket Press, 1987), p, 83.

[35] But see Philippians 2:9, "Therefore God exalted him to the highest place and gave him the name that is above every name, that at the name of Jesus every knee should bow, in heaven and on earth and under the earth, and every tongue acknowledge that Jesus Christ is Lord, to the glory of God the Father." Cf. Isaiah 45:23; Romans 14:10-11.

[36] For a classic, pre-Christian philosophical exploration of this dilemma, see Plato's *Euthyphro*.

Divine. Jesus is humble to the end, the definitive symbol of courage, power and wisdom. His reign never ceases. His glory never fades.

One complaint by several contemporary atheist writers regarding morality is, "the preposterous idea that we need God to be good."[37] Sam Harris, for example, believes that atheism gears us to scale the mountaintops of morality, while "religion" (a category some atheists apply to virtually anything they find ridiculous, repulsive or repugnant) leads to death and squalor. In *The Moral Landscape*, Harris argues for a utilitarian (the greatest happiness of the greatest number) or consequentialist ethic, but fails to demonstrate how any universal ethic, let alone a utilitarian one, can be derived from or is entailed by atheism. Atheists recount some motivations for moral behavior, describe examples and manifestations of morality and moral intuitions, but they do not, and perhaps cannot, supply an original source, authority or absolute adjudicator for moral principle, outrage and conviction. Is philosophical incoherence the price for denying a source for absolute morals?

Atheists, like Harris, can agree that Hitler was horribly wrong, but as the little girl asked the pastor in the movie, *Time Changer*, "Says who?"[38] Who or what is the final judge or moral appeal given atheism? Is it individual preference? Majority vote? Might makes right? A local or universal governing body? How does the atheist consistently answer and address the pithy maxim, "What is popular is not always right, and what is right is not always popular?"

If only there were someone with impeccable insight, who saw the whole picture, who weighed all the facts and considerations with boundless wisdom and blessed us with just the right amount of guidance in light of all other necessary considerations through our conscience,

---

37   Richard Dawkins in Sam Harris, The Moral Landscape (NY: Free Press, 2010), dust jacket. Cf. Benjamin B. DeVan, "Moral Landscapes or Sandscapes? New Atheist Grounds for Ethics and Morality,"*Books & Culture* (October, 2011), http://www.booksandculture.com/articles/webexclusives/2011/october/moral-landscapes.html, accessed November 1, 2011.
38   Time Changer (Christiano Film Group, 2002).

through written instructions or by exemplifying or incarnating wisdom for "how should we then live," to employ Francis Schaeffer's famous phrase.[39] But atheism rejects these options.

I applaud exemplars and exhortations to integrity by everyone, including atheists. But in my opinion, no atheist writer has yet successfully established why and how objective morality exists without an Ultimate Source of Morality. Atheist lauders and pursuers of truth, integrity and beauty can be none too careful. They might provoke or experience longings for the fountain of all Beauty, Goodness and Truth. Agnostic Robert Jastrow in *God and the Astronomers* uses the mountaintop metaphor to lament how probing the deepest mysteries of life might bring atheist and agnostic self-assured scientists unwittingly face to face with (to once again modify *Lord of the Rings*) the unlikeliest persons imaginable to them:

> It seems as though science will never…raise the curtain on the mystery of creation. For the scientist who has lived by his faith in the power of reason, the story ends like a bad dream. He has scaled the mountains of ignorance; he is about to conquer the highest peak; as he pulls himself over the final rock, he is greeted by a band of theologians who have been sitting there for centuries.[40]

Conclusion

The ethics and morality found within Hyrule help us understand and make sense of the quest to understand right and wrong in our own

---

39   Francis A. Schaeffer, How Shall We Then Live? The Rise and Decline of *Western Thought and Culture* (Francis Schaeffer 1976, Fleming H. Revell, 1979, 50th L'Abri Anniversary Edition, IL: Crossway Books, 2005).
40   Robert Jastrow, God and the Astronomers: New and Expanded Edition (Canada: Reader's Library, 1992), p. 107.

world, which, as the Christian believes, cannot be separated from the one who created us.

I don't envision theologians waiting at Jastrow's summit. I foresee the one who, "Gave life to everything that was created, and his life brought light to everyone" (John 1:4-5). Like Link and his shield, may we take up our cross, experiencing joyful surprise with fellow travelers at how the Grand Designer uses "earthen vessels," like young men and maidens, old men and children, mythic maps and fantasy games, to gesture to and open our eyes to the One who waits, calls and lifts us to the highest peaks of moral character, wisdom and abundant life.[41]

---

41   Scriptures alluded to in this paragraph include Psalm 148; Matthew 15:24; Mark 8:34; Luke 1:27; John 10:10; 1 Corinthians 12:4-7; 2 Corinthians 4, Galatians 2:19-20, 5:22-23; Philippians 2:12-13; James 1:2-5; Hebrews 4:16.

Portals, Prophecy and Cuccos: Considerations of Power in A Link to the Past

Jeremy Smith

As a child, one of my first lessons in ethics came from a chicken in *The Legend of Zelda: A Link to the Past*.[1] In the game, there are chickens called cuccos running around and I would laugh at its cries of fear while swatting them with my sword. One day I was showing my brother this hilarity when, unexpectedly, a hundred cuccos stormed on screen pecking mercilessly at me as they flew by. In an unfortunate coincidence, I was down to one or two hearts of life energy at the time and, to my childhood horror, actually died as a result of my cucco torment. It was a harsh lesson: don't mess with the cucco...or at least don't mess with them too much.

It's also a lesson on ethics because the scenario with the cucco is a question of how to use one's power. The *Zelda* universe is primarily a story about good v. evil, of course; but more specifically, it is a story about the use of power. One of the iconic artifacts in the Zelda universe is the Triforce: three interlocked triangles that grant the bearer significant power. The protagonist Link thus embarks on the hero's journey from powerless to merely underpowered compared to the antagonist Ganon.

The ethical considerations of the use of power are a persistent theme in the *Zelda* series, in general, and *Link to the Past*, in particular. In engaging this topic, *LttP* contains numerous references to the Christian journey and the role of power in our everyday lives. Much of Christian theology is about good and evil, certainly, but also the use of power: the power of Christ to break the chains of sin, the power of Christians to overcome injustice and oppression, the restrictions placed on Christians in authority, etc.

Through examining the hero's journey in this story, the role of power comes to the forefront: what does power do to corrupt or purify

---

1   *The Legend of Zelda: A Link to the Past*. Nintendo of America, Redmond, WA. 1992. Super Nintendo. English.

one's desires? We will outline three problems of this particular world that serve as lenses to our own ethical behavior in the analog world.

Problem One: A Choice Issue

First, there is the problem of choice. Like Neo in the movie *The Matrix*,[2] who realized that there was a choice to save Morpheus or disconnect him from the Matrix, thus killing him, every hero's journey involves the hero making choices and dealing with the consequences. Video games, as a medium, offer a unique arena in which to explore and experience the phenomenon of "choice," unmatched by any other form of art.

These choices become more complex when they effect change in parallel universes. A "parallel universe" is a plot element introduced in *A Link to the Past* that becomes part of most of the subsequent *Zelda* stories. The parallel universes in this story are the Light world (reality) and the Dark world (a twisted parallel universe ruled by Ganon) and changes in one area are reflected in the other.

When Link defeats Agahnim (a wicked wizard) and is sent to the Dark World, the Sage Sahasrahla says the following:

> In order to save this world, the Light World, you must win back the Golden Power.[3]

It may be a shock to readers that Sahasrahla expresses no interest whatsoever in saving the inhabitants of the Dark World and perhaps portrays them as irredeemable because their world will be destroyed anyway. The maiden in the Ice Temple (and the Essence of the Triforce at the end of the game) expresses the same sentiment: *"If you defeat Ganon, this world [the Dark World] will vanish..."* In fact, Sahasrahla wants Link in

---

2   *The Matrix*. Dir. The Wachoski Bros. Perf. Keanu Reeves and Laurence Fishburne. DVD. Warner, 1999.

3   Ibid *The Legend of Zelda*.

the Dark World only to save the maidens because they were taken there by force and not twisted by choice. The Dark World, according to them, is Ganon's creation and has no redeeming value.

And yet there are many people in the Dark World who may be twisted versions of their Light World selves but are still redeemable and can be helped by Link. Often, they are not found in the Light World at all but are redeemed through Link's actions. For example, the Swordsmith in the Light World considers his partner hopelessly lost, but his partner is found in the Dark World and returned to him through Link's actions. There is also the Flute Boy who is twisted by his own choices but is redeemed by Link's action in the Dark World. As a result, he disappears and has what appears to be a peaceful end after hearing his Ocarina "one...last...time." These characters are not always necessary to Link's quest, but they are all shown as redeemed in the end credits sequence. The hero, therefore, has to choose whether to help in these side quests or to disregard them on his journey to the ultimate prize.

Christian theologians throughout the ages have pontificated on the problem of choice and the ethical conundrums of the use of power in decision-making and rule. We have the same problem of choice today. Every dollar in our hand could buy a Big Mac, adopt a child, put a well in a village, teach a lesson of responsibility to a child, feed a homeless person, be gambled in a casino or be tithed to a church. People with real power in the real world are given dictates by the Bible on how to use their power justly,[4] people without power are given advice on how to hold themselves with dignity and grace[5] and people in-between are given clear instructions on priorities and choices.[6]

But, most importantly, is the choice of worldview: If the Dark World is going to pass away, if this mortal coil is going to be "Left Behind"

---

4   Psalm 82, Romans 9, NRSV.
5   The Book of Daniel, an apocalyptic Hebrew Bible text.
6   Matthew 25:40, NRSV.

(as in Revelation's biblical vision[7]), why do any good at all? Why spend time saving people who don't matter? We'll come back to this choice later.

In the meantime, it is most telling that the person who wants to *limit* "who is saved" is Sahasrahla, a Sage who is of the religious establishment. Conversely, can we think of anyone who, like Link, *expanded* the dictates of "who is to be saved" beyond the religious establishment? Can we think of anyone who expanded his role beyond the original intent and included more in his mission? For the people of Israel at the time of Jesus Christ, they expected their Messiah to be a conquering hero who would vindicate the Temple and subjugate everyone non-Israelite under their feet. But Jesus Christ embraced his role as the Messiah, not merely as a conquering hero for Israel, but also as the Redeemer of the entire world, non-Israelites included. Doubtlessly, Link is no Jesus, but Link does choose to reinterpret and expand his ascribed role for the betterment of all humankind, like Jesus did.

Problem 2: Who Knows Which is Which and Who is Who?

Second, there is the problem of how to differentiate between the sources of good and evil. In the *LttP* game, this revolves around portals. The maiden in the Water Temple (ugh, I hate that level) explains:

> There are some other magical warping points like the one you saw on Death Mountain. By using them you can go between the two worlds and find the evils hidden in the Dark World.[8]

In *LttP*, one transcends these universes through the use of portals that Link steps on to warp between the Light World and the Dark World.

---

7   The Revelation to John, the apocalyptic last book of the Christian New Testament.

8   Ibid *The Legend of Zelda.*

Portals, Prophecy and Cuccos: Considerations of Power in A Link to the Past

The similarity between the two parallel universes of the Light World and the Dark World is striking: Buildings are in the same places, landscapes look identical with merely a palette swap and cuccos in one world become monstrous skeletal hens in the next. These portals allow Link to combat Ganon in both light and dark worlds and transporting between worlds is often the only way to solve particular puzzles.

In theological conversation, perhaps real-life portals are "thin places" where the divine world and our tangible world meet or are seen most clearly. Ancient Celtic Christians in Ireland, from the 20th century Trappist monk Thomas Merton up to contemporary theologian Marcus Borg, write about this concept in varying ways. While Celts primarily focus on places of nature and unspoiled mountaintops as thin places, Merton expands on this understanding:

> God shows [God's] self everywhere, in everything—in people and in things and in nature and in events. It becomes very obvious that God is everywhere and in everything and we cannot be without [God]. It's impossible. The only thing is that we don't see it.[9]

Borg outlines the gamut of Christian practices to be primarily about opening up our awareness to God through "thin places" which can be physical locations, liturgies, music, actions and people:

> Music, poetry, literature, the visual arts, and dance can all become thin places in which the boundary between one's self and the world momentarily disappears.[10]

Merton and Borg both see thin places as everyday moments when the break between the divine and the profane is healed for a moment.

---

9   T. Merton. Audiotape, 1965. Quoted in M. Borg. *The Heart of Christianity*. HarperCollins, 2004. 155.

10   Ibid, 156.

Perhaps teaching a homeless person a marketable skill resulting in the person feeling worthy of God's love is a thin place. Perhaps selfless giving of food to transients without hope of boosted church attendance is a thin place. A pastor offering unexpectedly helpful words to a teenager who had an abortion is, perhaps, a thin place. These moments are found in the everyday and are important elements to spiritual growth and bringing forth the kingdom of God here on earth.

Perhaps instead of thin places being Celtic locations of perfect peace with God, they are places where our light/dark sides are most intimately connected. In *LttP*, portals are located in dangerous sections of the light world, such as mountaintops or in the middle of lakes. So the two worlds meet, not in solitude, but in the very midst of the fight for freedom.

In *LttP*, only by choosing to engage the Dark World is change effected in the Light World. Draining the lake in the Light World allows entrance into the fearsome Water Temple. Saving the flute boy (who has been written off by Sahasrahla) yields entrance to the impassable Swamp Temple. Perhaps, then, we are most connected to the divine, not through the disengagement of mountain sanctuaries, but through engagement with the thin places of the world, seeking justice for the oppressed and witnessing to the transformational power of Christ in the darkest of alleys.

Like Link's choice to save those who have been forsaken, perhaps we also are to seek the portals, find the thin places where God and the world meet most dramatically and reside there, seeking wholeness on the wrong side of the right world.

Problem 3: Tipping the Golden Mean

Third, and most importantly, is the problem that springs from the goal of ethical behavior: the Triforce itself. Any serious study of *Zelda* has to address this powerful entity. Every saved maiden says, "May the way of the hero lead to the Triforce," and every *Zelda* game is culminated via the Triforce in some way. In many *Zelda* titles, the Triforce is split into three entities that most reflect their bearer's personality: Power (Ganon),

Portals, Prophecy and Cuccos: Considerations of Power in A Link to the Past

Wisdom (Zelda) and Courage (Link). In *LttP*, the Triforce is already whole in the Dark World, perhaps leading one to think it would be a form of power that grants its total authority to the bearer, but that's not quite how *LttP* puts it. Here's the Sage Sahasrahla again:

> The Triforce...grant[s] the wishes in the heart and mind of whoever touches it.

At the end of the game, the Essence of the Triforce expounds on that topic:

> The Triforce will grant the wishes in the heart and mind of the person who touches it. If a person with a good heart touches it, it will make his good wishes come true. If an evil-hearted person touches it, it grants his evil wishes.[11]

In other words, the Triforce is concerned with the nature of one's heart. Good hearts yield good wishes, bad hearts yield bad wishes.

The ethical conundrum emerges if we take the description literally (which, like many Biblical passages and metaphors, may or may not be the correct approach). The Triforce seems to be concerned with tipping points. If a person is mostly good, his good wishes are granted when he touches the Triforce. If he is mostly bad, his bad wishes are granted. This is an ethical problem because a good person can do *some* bad things to obtain the Triforce's power, so long as he is mostly good. Along the way, the hero could have swatted a few cuccos but still have enough good in his heart to tip the Triforce to grant good wishes.

To state the problem another way, the Triforce seems to embrace a teleological ethical viewpoint: the "ends justify the means."[12] This philosophy holds that the ends (*telos*) of an action are the sole judge of

---
11   Ibid *The Legend of Zelda*
12   Also called *consequentialism,* popularized by a range of philosophers ie. Jeremy Bentham, John Stuart Mill, etc.

its goodness, not the means by which one obtains it. This philosophy is strikingly similar to a well-known worldview commonly known as Consequentialism, known for its extremely pragmatic take on ethics: The more people who experience the good, the better. Never mind the method. As far as the Triforce is concerned, if a person has a good heart, he can do bad things, so long as his actions do not overwhelm his heart. For example, missionaries in Haiti could abduct children over the border because they were offering them a better life.[13] Hell Houses in the Bible Belt could scare children to Jesus through violent imagery.[14] To these situations, the ends supposedly justify the means because the "good" outcome (in their minds) outweighs the flawed methods. This question of methods and means as opposed to ends and goals is an essential ethical question for people to address.

Which Link to the Past?

A Link to the Past offers a powerful lens to examine the role of power in our own lives and a potent way to explain theological concepts to nerds and gamer girls, but all of this discussion of the elements of power leaves us wanting a framework for the conversation. Every *Zelda* game is a story that is being told and the ethical use of power is an integral element or chapter in the story. So what is the story being told in *LttP*? And what is the story in which we can wrap our considerations of power and make some sort of sense?

There is one barely mentioned, but very important, story element to *LttP* that offers clarity on this topic. Even though the Triforce is powerful, there is a built-in check to the Power of the Triforce: the Great Cataclysm. The maiden in the Dark World dungeon in the Skull Forest explains the

---

13   A. Butler, "Missionary Imposition: Idaho Baptists Charged With Kidnapping 33 Haitian Children" Internet Document, 2010. <http://www.religiondispatches.org/archive/politics/2257/>.

14   J. Smith. "Hell Houses" Internet Document, 2009. <http://hackingchristianity.net/2009/10/hell-houses.html>.

Great Cataclysm:

> If a person who has an evil heart gets the Triforce, a Hero is destined to appear and he alone must face the person who unleashed the Great Cataclysm. If the evil one destroys the Hero, nothing can save the world from his wicked reign.[15]

Thus the power of the Triforce has a failsafe: If a person with an evil heart obtains it, then eventually someone could take him out. Balance is thus restorable, evil is undoable, treachery is reversible, but only in the fullness of time and only through one single being. (This just so happens to be you, which makes for a great video game!)

As in *LTTP*, it seems that when our world is out of sorts, God has built a failsafe into it. It is the Christ, the one who comes in the fullness of time to set things right, leaving us to interpret which kind of failsafe it is.

- **Is Christ a *cataclysmic* Christ** who ushers in an era of Good v. Evil, culminating in the final days of fire, destruction of this dark world and redemption of the "worthy" into the Golden Realm... er, Heaven? This is the Triumphant Christ of Sahasrahla, who sees the spiritual struggle and wants nothing but to vanquish all things dark, as the legend tells. We need to save the lost souls at all costs, but let the rest of the world and any environmental sensibilities be damned to hell, because it is all going to be destroyed anyway.
- **Or is Christ a *catalytic* Christ** who comes at just the right moment to spur humanity, whose story is still being played out, in a different direction which he could have chosen before but did not? This is the Compassionate Christ emulated by Link, who acknowledges the spiritual struggle but does not allow this to interfere with helping individuals and expanding the circle of God's grace to people beyond. The end of this age will surely

---

15   Ibid.

come but, in the meantime, by helping all whom you meet, you can make even the darkest of worlds into a place of God's grace. These are two very different Christs. And their conflict is found in most of today's hot topics. Do we preserve the earth God created for us or accept that it will be burned up in the Second Coming? Do we do justice work with unbelievers or leave those who reject salvation to the sidelines? Humans have immense power in either worldview. The key questions is: What does Christ mean to the world and how are we to interpret the story of Christianity as expressed in the scriptures? Do we hold to it literally, like Sahasrahla and the Pharisees (the cataclysmic view)? Or do we allow God's grace to be free of human constraints and express itself in new and remarkable ways (the catalytic view)?[16] We end up where we began with the problem of choice and this is a large choice that influences smaller choices down the line.

Conclusion

In more than one instance, cuccos taught me an ethical lesson. One of the Easter Eggs (hidden surprises) in the game is that if you sprinkle your magic powder on the Cucco found under a jar in one of the Light World townhouses, it becomes a human woman and chastises you:

> Ah-ha! You must be the one who is always teasing my friends. The Weathervane has seen you harass them... Cluck cluck...

The large, all-seeing eye that knows when you sin and knows when you offer grace is a judge of sorts in this world. Also note that the symbol of Agahnim's dark reign is an eye, while the Weathervane in the town square is topped, not with an eye, but with the wooden bird that breaks upon hearing its song and returns to carry you around Hyrule. The all-seeing

---

16   Acts 11, NRSV.

sculpture erected by people long ago is broken and given new life when it hears a song it recognizes and takes the player to greater heights.

Perhaps we also stand before our judge with a sword and an Ocarina in our hand. Which will we use? Will our judge hear the cries of a cucco being swatted by the sword? Or will our judge hear the Ocarina that brings more music into the world? Will we use our power for self-satisfaction or to set free that which is beautiful, wherever we might be?

The choice is yours.

The Necessity of the Triforce in the Defeat of Ganon

D.M. Burke

The explosion echoes off the surrounding rock face, each iteration diminishing into the distance. Wiping dust off of his tunic, he looks with satisfaction at the yawning opening before him. "Time to end this," he thinks grimly. He makes his way through the first chamber, decorated with the same grotesque statues that marked other vanquished dungeons. He takes a moment to collect himself, tired from the battle with the Lynels surrounding the mammoth boulder that marks the entrance to Ganon's lair. Peering into the second room, he sees a wizened figure seated between two tongues of flame that seem to hover just above the obsidian surface of the floor. The withered form stirs as Link enters the room. The old man raises his head and fixes surprisingly lucid eyes on Link's own. "Without the Triforce, you may not pass." It is a simple statement spoken almost casually. It's not threatening or ominous, just a simple fact. The six pieces of the Triforce of Wisdom already in Link's possession glow momentarily as if in agreement. Sudden understanding floods through Link. "I can't do this on my own, only the completed Triforce can defeat Ganon," he murmurs quietly. The old man nods once and resumes his reverie. Link hitches his shield a little higher on his back, turns around and heads back out into the sunlight.

The original *Legend of Zelda* continues to be one of my all-time favorite games. It was the first game I ever encountered that provided an epic and fleshed out storyline of good versus evil. Link was a different order of hero from Mario, Pac-Man or the unnamed starship captain from *Space Invaders*. There was something more serious about his quest and the seemingly greater repercussions for failure. For a fan of epic fantasy from the likes of J.R.R. Tolkien and C.S. Lewis, *The Legend of Zelda* was a choose-your-own-adventure dream come true. Not only did it provide a deeper storyline than I was used to, it was sufficiently non-linear so that it gave the game an immensity that I'd never before experienced.

For those of you who never had the pleasure of the original, but fell in love with later *Zelda* titles, the preface to the beginning of the game runs thus: Ganon, the Prince of Darkness, has stolen the Triforce of Power, a mystical triangular talisman, and is using it to conquer the land of Hyrule in order to possess the Triforce of Wisdom as well. His ultimate aim is to use the power of these mystical items to plunge the world into chaos and darkness. Princess Zelda broke the Triforce of Wisdom into eight pieces and hid them across the land of Hyrule. Ganon, furious with being thwarted, imprisoned Zelda. However, before her imprisonment, Zelda sent her nursemaid away to find a hero to come to Hyrule and defeat Ganon. While fleeing, the nursemaid is surrounded by Ganon's henchmen and things are looking grim when a young boy appears and saves the nursemaid's life. On hearing her tale, he resolves to go to Hyrule and defeat Ganon. The game itself consists of Link, whose strength of sword arm and the beneficence of mysterious (but friendly) strangers, fights his way through the eight dungeons in which the pieces of the Triforce are guarded in order to gain the Triforce of Wisdom and defeat Ganon, the Prince of Darkness.

    Hours and hours into my first adventure, having found and defeated the enemies of the first six levels, I remember stumbling across the entrance to level nine, which I knew to be Ganon's stronghold and thus the end of the game. Even though I hadn't defeated levels seven and eight, I defiantly walked Link into the dungeon, intent on bringing an early demise to Ganon. I admit to being furiously annoyed upon being turned back because I hadn't successfully collected all pieces of the Triforce. Was I not a confident warrior who had vanquished foes of the overworld and dungeons alike? Had I not defeated mighty dungeon bosses, like the great dragon Aquamentus and the dinosaur-like Dodongo? Did I not have the blue protection ring and magical sword at my disposal and vast numbers of hearts to protect me from defeat? What was this mystical triangular stone that was necessary for me to banish the Prince of Darkness from Hyrule?

    What I couldn't know at the time is that once Link enters

The Necessity of the Triforce in the Defeat of Ganon

Ganon's chamber, he raises the Triforce of Wisdom high, which provides the light by which he is able to defeat Ganon. I imagine that, had the old man at the entrance let Link through without the Triforce, he would have been defeated by the impenetrable darkness of the chamber and the evil power of the Prince of Darkness.

Years later, reflecting on my disappointment at being thwarted from achieving an early victory, and having developed a much greater appreciation for the truths that underlie Story, I came to realize a vital reality that is reflected in Link's quest and the necessity of the Triforce for Ganon's defeat: in order to defeat evil, or for even the ability to define evil, something transcendent, something outside of ourselves, something beyond the physical world, is necessary.

Transcendence and the Ability to Define Evil

We are very comfortable with the idea of "sides" in video games. There are very few[1] (if any) games out there in which the player is not able to immediately identify, in some way, with the character he is playing. When we identify with the character, we are immediately able to understand that this is "my" side which is "good" and another side which is "evil." Reading through *The Legend of Zelda's* game manual, we see that Link, upon hearing the story of Ganon's attack on Hyrule, is "burning with a sense of justice" and that he "resolved to save Zelda."[2] Link is immediately a good and heroic figure and Ganon is immediately the "evil enemy." It doesn't help Ganon's case that he also is labeled "The Prince of Darkness." But how is it that Link is able to immediately peg Ganon's actions as evil and resolve to undo this wickedness?

---

1   It is worth noting the new type of game that allows players to choose "evil" choices and to follow an "evil" path with their characters. Even in these situations, the player is aware the he is willfully enacting the wrong rather than the right and good. Also, in morally ambiguous games such as Mass Effect and Heavy Rain, the player still feels a strong sense of identity with his character and views his side of the fight as "right" and "good"

2   *The Legend of* Zelda, Nintendo of America, 1987, instruction booklet, pg.

Further, why do we so easily accept Link as the hero and eagerly take part in defeating this injustice? Put more broadly, how is it that human beings can even make judgments that something is actually good or evil?

One way to make sense of the moral categories of good and evil is to appeal to group or societal consensus. This view basically says that categories of good and evil are created through mutually agreed upon goals or ideals for a group of people and "evil" is anything that hinders or goes against those goals or ideals. The problem with this view is that if there are two groups or societies with conflicting viewpoints, it becomes difficult for one to decide which is good and which is evil. To illustrate this point, let's consider Ganon's point of view. He and his armies appear to have a serious problem with the land of Hyrule. We are left to imagine what that problem might be as the opening storyline only tells us that Ganon desires to plunge the world into darkness and chaos, but I think one can safely assume that Ganon's worldview provides him with reasons for these actions. Perhaps he has sensitive eyes and skin and thus wishes that the sun didn't shine quite so brightly. Perhaps he is an anarchist at heart who believes kingdoms and feudal systems should be expunged so everyone can learn to fend for themselves and, thus, become stronger. Or maybe Ganon loves darkness, chaos and evil for its own sake. Whatever his reasons for invading Hyrule, he must have one with which his followers also essentially agree. On top of that, he feels sufficiently passionate enough about it to destroy an entire kingdom and its population to achieve it.

Diametrically opposed to Ganon are Zelda and Link. Their worldview apparently does not relish the idea of darkness and chaos and they are willing to risk their lives to make sure that Ganon doesn't accomplish his goals. From outside the game, we very easily side with Link, as our cultural and historical values tend to fall very much in line with freedom, light and order. But what if there *were* no "outside the game"? Inside the world of *Zelda*, how can an objective observer determine which side is truly "good" and which is "evil"? Further, it could be argued that in the world of *Zelda*, there are no objective observers, just those that have been culturally and historically raised to align with one viewpoint over the other. If societal consensus based on cultural and historical values is the standard of what is good and evil, the final word comes down to which side achieves victory, either expunging all of those with contrary views or changing the minds of the conquered. There is no real way to adjudicate which side is right and which is wrong. To be sure, this view that morality is simply societal consensus is logically consistent but, if that is true, we have to give up on the idea that morality is objective (not defined by preference) and binding upon all persons.

Another way of justifying morality is to appeal to evolutionary concepts.[3] This view says that survival of the species, even above survival of the individual, is the aim of existence. Morality, the ability to define and distinguish between good and evil, is just an evolutionarily beneficial trait that allows the survival of the human species. Most societies (if not all) have some sort of prohibition against murder. To be sure, there are times when killing another human being is justified in the framework of almost any society, but wanton murder, killing for revenge, killing to take from another or killing for personal pleasure are generally considered evil.

The evolutionary approach would claim that this prohibition is hardwired into our brains and is merely a biological trait that protects us from destroying our species. On the surface, this view seems to make a lot of sense. A bloodthirsty species that is hell-bent on killing other members of its own species doesn't seem like a good candidate for long-term survival. While this adds up when thinking about the species as a whole, there are several problems that arise when applying it to the individual.

If we think about Link's actions in this framework, his protection of the nursemaid is not really a heroic action, nor is his determination

---

[3] Friedrich Nietzsche touches on this idea while championing nature as the standard of behavior: Friedrich Nietzsche, *Beyond Good and Evil*, trans. Marion Faber (New York: Oxford University Press, 1998).

to take on Ganon. Rather, because it is hard-wired into his biology, it just "is." Let's consider an alternate storyline. What if Link, confronted with Ganon's henchmen attacking the poor nursemaid, had joined in the fray on their side, hoping to split the spoils with them? Under a biological view of morality, could we really call his actions evil? In this scenario, Link would simply be missing whatever genetic trait is supposed to make him concerned about the survival of a member of his species. We might consider him "defective," but there is no room for a value judgment because Link, due to his biological makeup, could not have behaved differently. Now, imagine you were standing in the woods witnessing Link's attack on an innocent. You might not like Link's actions, but again, in this framework, that is merely due to your biological makeup, which has determined you to feel moral outrage. Under this view, nature is the source of all actions, as well as the source of how we feel about those actions, but there is no objective way to provide a moral definition, there is just personal preference. The categories of good and evil, in this view, become meaningless as each of us simply fulfills the functions that were set in place at birth.

So what are we to make of the concepts of good and evil if they don't come from society or nature? If that's the case, morality must have a source outside of us and outside of nature. It must have a transcendent[4] basis. In fairness, there are various transcendental bases for morality. Each religious system that claims a divine power has a framework that provides the foundation for good and evil. Further, Immanuel Kant argues for a morality from pure reason[5] (which can be

---

4   "Transcendent" as used here is the opposite of immanent: immanent is that which is within us such as our thoughts and preferences or the physical world that is around us. Transcendent is that which is beyond the tangible world.

5   "Morality, just as much as mathematics and natural science, is constituted in part by *a priori* elements originating in the nature of reason itself. Therefore it is necessary to work out 'a pure moral philosophy that is wholly cleared of everything which can only be empirical and can only belong to anthropology.' In pursuing such a philosophy, Kant is engaged in nothing less than 'seeking

viewed as transcendent) and John Stewart Mill argues for a morality based on the greatest good for the greatest number[6] (which also could be considered a transcendent basis). There are hundreds of books and thousands of arguments that address the foundations, merits and flaws of all of these views, but here we will focus on the Christian view, which claims that this transcendent foundation is the Trinitarian God of the Bible.

In the Christian worldview, God is not only outside of our normal physical existence, He is the author and creator of reality.[7] "Reality" here is defined not only as the physical world, but also all that is in it. It's important to note that reality adheres to laws of physics, mathematics, logic and morality that reflect the eternal nature and mind of God. So God did not merely craft a physical world, He essentially also imbued it with a framework in which the physical and material exist. It makes sense then that the kind of existence that was created tells us about the kind of God He is. The creation of humanity is telling in that it points to a God who is personal, that is, interested in relationships. It doesn't make much sense for creation, especially humanity, to be so concerned with relationships to one another[8] and relationship to the Divine[9] (which is common to most of humanity throughout history) if this did not reflect the intention of the Creator. (Granted, there are other reasonable explanations for why humanity is relational outside of the Christian worldview, but I am arguing from within this worldview.)

---

out and establishing the supreme principle of morality.'" Norman Melchert, *The Great Conversation: Volume 2, Heidegger through Descartes*, (Mountain View, CA: Mayfield Publishing Company, 1995), 402. For further reading, see Immanuel Kant, *Grounding for the Metaphysics of Morals*, trans. James W Ellington (Indianapolis: Hackett Publishing Co., 1982).

6   John Stuart Mill, *Utilitarianism*, ed. George Sher (Indianapolis: Hackett Publishing Co., 1979)

7   Genesis Chapter 1

8   Genesis 2:18-24, Mark 12:28-34

9   Deuteronomy 6:1-9

Notice that in *The Legend of Zelda,* the story and game itself provide positive relationships: Link finds helpful people in his journey and, in the end, he personally rescues Zelda, which hints at the uniting or reuniting of a romantic relationship common in so many stories. Further, God chose to reveal Himself to humanity through nature (natural or general revelation) and through communicating with specific people throughout history (special revelation).[10] And as we see in Scripture, God is also very interested in how human beings relate to Him and to one another.[11] So, Christians would argue that since the origin of morality is from God, definitions of good and evil are not open to the subjectivity of societal views or the "just is"-ness of nature. They are, rather, built into the very fabric of reality and binding upon all of creation.

It is not enough, however, to simply assert that morality derives from a transcendent being. It is also important to understand the nature of that morality as to how it defines good and evil. This begins with understanding the nature of the Christian God and, therefore, understanding the Trinity. Christian doctrine asserts that God is one being but three persons. Much ink has been spilt throughout history on this concept[12] and there is not space enough here to go in depth on this idea, so it must be put succinctly: There are three distinct aspects to God: the Father, the Son and the Holy Spirit. This means that, before creation, God existed in relationship among the persons of the Trinity. The

---

10   "Special revelation" is the means by which God has made his will and personality known to humanity by revealing himself to specific human beings throughout history such as the prophets and other figures as seen in the stories of the Bible as well as the apex of revelation in Jesus Christ who was fully God and fully human and revealed the nature of God to humanity through his life, teachings, death and resurrection.

11   It is instructive to read the laws of the book of Deuteronomy with this principle in mind.

12   For further reading on the doctrine of the Holy Spirit see Thomas C. Oden, *Life in the Spirit: Systematic Theology: Volume Three* (Peabody, MA: Prince Press, 2001).

Father existed in loving relationship with the Son and Holy Spirit, the Son existed in loving relationship with the Father and Holy Spirit and the Holy Spirit existed in loving relationship with the Father and Son. This is vital because it allows for loving relationship to be an irreducible aspect of the nature of God; that is, God did not require anything outside of Himself to have the attribute of loving relationship.

    We, then, see in the book of Genesis in the Bible that ==God created humanity to be in loving relationship with Himself.== This was not some mental assertion or random decision on the part of God, but rather an act based on His fundamental nature. Further, God did not create humanity as a pet or slave but imbued humanity with the very image of God. This meant that humanity, and indeed each individual, was created to bear the likeness of God in moral and intellectual capacity, the ability to reason, etc. As a result, ==each person has value because each is a reflection of how God values each person.== This helps us, then, to understand the categories of good and evil. "Good" is that which recognizes the value of humans as being created in God's image and, further, ==good is anything that fosters loving relationship with God and among humanity.== On the flip side, evil is that which denigrates or destroys the value of humanity and impedes loving relationship with God or among humans. This is why we heartily cheer Link on to rescue Zelda's nursemaid and detest Ganon's henchmen for their ill intentions. We, and Link, recognize the inherent value in her.

    Understanding that God created humanity based on His own nature and meant humanity to be in loving relationship with Himself and one another provides a much clearer lens through which to view the rules of behavior that God handed down through natural and special revelation.

    In terms of natural revelation, C.S. Lewis, in *The Abolition of Man*, points out that the moral intuitions of humanity throughout time appear to have a high degree of similarity.[13] The moral values of humanity

---

13   C.S. Lewis, *The Abolition of Man* (New York, NY: Harper Collins, 2001),

have a fundamental basis, which Lewis calls the *Tao*.[14] He argues that this, at least, seems to point to the fact that doing good to others and not doing harm is present in humanity's deepest intuitions provided to us by our nature. "This thing which I have called for convenience the *Tao*, and which others may call Natural Law or Traditional Morality or the First Principles of Practical Reason or the First Platitudes, is not one among a series of possible systems of value. It is the sole source of all value judgments."[15] If it is true that the goal of life is to be in loving relationship with God and one another, then it stands to reason that all created beings share a basic sense of right and wrong and this manifests in generally the same way, regardless of cultural and historical differences.

Regarding special revelation, there is much in the Bible that can be difficult to attribute to Christian morality, which can be defined as a loving relationship with God and humanity. For example, think about such outdated and seemingly absurd laws, like the prohibition against boiling a kid in its mother's milk, or laws regarding what to do when mold is growing inside one's house. Here the problem is our tremendous historical and cultural distance from the time such laws came about, which leaves us completely unable to assess how they played into fundamental morality. For example, someone from outside the land of Hyrule may find it morally abhorrent that Link blithely kills every mobllin he sees but, since we take this story at face value, we simply accept that there must be some deep enmity or assumption of evil inherent in mobllins. However, many other laws from the Old Testament, as well as much of the teaching of Jesus and the writings of New Testament figures, provide a very clear picture that God is ultimately concerned with how we relate to Him and each other. In

---

14-19; 83-101.

14   C.S. Lewis, *The Abolition of Man* (New York, NY: Harper Collins, 2001), 18.

15   Ibid., 43

fact, most, if not all, of Jesus' teachings were focused on being in loving relationship with those around us, and many Old Testament laws, such as building a railing around the roof of your house[16] (which was a place one used to entertain guests) show the intensely practical focus of God's revelation on the well-being of humanity (you are responsible for protecting others from falling off your roof).

So if the underlying reality of creation itself is loving relationship with God and one another, then we are able to identify what is objectively good (anything that fosters loving relationship with God and among humanity and/or enhances the value of human beings) and what is objectively evil (anything that hinders loving relationship with God and among humanity and/or degrades the value of human beings). This is not to say that loving relationships or being kind towards others is a uniquely Christian concept or that Christians always practice this and others don't. There are many who do not claim to be Christians who are quite moral and loving and there are many Christians who are bigoted and hateful. The point here is that a transcendental foundation that is based upon the nature of God provides us with the ability to define these behaviors as good or evil regardless of the purported worldview of the one doing the behavior.

The storyline of *The Legend of Zelda* tells us that Ganon has in his possession and is using the Triforce of Power and that Link must use the Triforce of Wisdom to enact his defeat. According to the previously mentioned sketches of morality based on societal consensus and morality based on evolutionary concepts, power can be an appropriate justification for actions as the victor or the majority define morality according to their views and desires. Thankfully for us, Link seeks out wisdom as his ally so we can join with him in wholeheartedly condemning Ganon's actions as evil.

---

16   Deuteronomy 22:8

Transcendence and the Ability to Defeat Evil

Now that we understand how we can rightly join with Link in desiring to fight for justice and defeat Ganon, let's consider his *ability* to defeat evil. Throughout his journey, Link continually improves his weaponry, his defenses and his personal strength, so why does he need the Triforce of Wisdom to defeat Ganon? In Link's world, Ganon is a representative of chaos and disorder. He is described as "the powerful Prince of Darkness who sought to plunge the World into fear and darkness under his rule.[17]" This description, understandably, resonates with players as we all have an inherent fear of disorder and darkness. In fact, this kind of enemy is a common element to many stories in and out of the video game world. Some of the earliest recorded stories of the human race, such as the Epic of Gilgamesh, portray evil as some manifestation of chaos and disorder that must be defeated or brought under control. It is also common for us to refer to someone we believe to be evil as having a "darkness" within them. But just what is it that these concepts of chaos and darkness are getting at?

The origins of evil throughout history are usually seen as coming from some outside evil force or personality and the Christian worldview is no exception. Evil entered into the world when the devil tempted Adam and Eve into being disobedient to God, thus causing a rift in the relationship between God and humanity, as well as between Adam and Eve. This rift in relationship, in Christian parlance, is known as sin. Remember from our earlier argument that this is the very definition of evil: anything that hinders loving relationship between God and humanity and among human beings. This, in short, is the doctrine of original sin. While classical Christian teaching does consider the devil to be present and active in this world, the main problem of evil in humanity

---

17 *The Legend of* Zelda, Nintendo of America, 1987, instruction booklet, pg. 3

is not that the devil does all the bad stuff, it is that humanity, because of our bad choices, has lost the ability to be in right relationship with God. As a result, we have free choice, but carry an inherent penchant for choosing evil rather than good. The dichotomous relationship between our good gift of free will and our bad, sinful nature is manifested clearly in two ways; namely, the sheer amount and variety of evil in the world and humanity's inability to reconcile its actions with its general desires to do good.

Dodongo would love to quit stomping around the room endangering the life of any wanderer attempting to cross, but it feels so darn good to run over those pesky intruders and squash them into the ground! Goriya would love to be a decent guy and let Link pass, but (grumble, grumble) he's so hungry! Nevermind that Link is trying to set the land of Hyrule free from an evil invader, a man's gotta eat! Basic, selfish desires often trump what we know to be the right thing to do in many everyday situations.

Enter the concept of total depravity. Total depravity is the concept that, because of original sin, we are separated from God and actually incapable of choosing the Good. No matter how much we want to do good rather than evil, our sinful nature prevents it. This depravity is so deep that, by ourselves, we are incapable of even choosing to be in relationship with God, (the only thing that can help us out of this state of affairs) which, in turn, prevents us from valuing and nurturing our relationships with those around us. To summarize total depravity, it is abject selfishness. It is the pursuit of one's desires and goals despite the repercussions to those around us. Defining evil in this way may tempt us to think that evil really isn't so bad after all because, while selfishness may be undesirable, taking a couple of rupees off someone isn't mass murder. Consider, though, that the difference between the small rupee theft and Ganon's invasion is a matter of scale and not of type. Both are motivated by the desire of an individual over the welfare of others.

If total depravity is true, what do we make of Link's selfless and heroic actions? How is he able to decide to undertake the defeat of Ganon? The good news (literally, as the word "gospel" is the Greek term for "good news") is that God, because He created us to be in loving relationship with Him and one another, does not leave us in this state, unable to choose good over evil. He freed us to be able to choose the Good through the life of Jesus Christ, his death on the cross and his resurrection. The life of Jesus, and the fact that he was fully human as well as fully divine, is absolutely essential because it first provides us with an example of the possibility of living a life of perfect love for God and one another. Jesus, by relying on the power of God, was able to continually and consistently choose good over evil. Without such an example, we might be tempted to think this impossible. The important point here is that it was through his relationship with God, not as God's Son but as a human being, that he was able to live life in this fashion. Devoid of a relationship with God, human beings are doomed to choose evil.

Just as important is the reality that Jesus, enabled by his full divinity, bore the deserved punishment (deserved by us) for the evil of all mankind. This punishment is death, which is the cessation of the ability to be in loving relationship with anyone or anything. And not only did he bear the punishment on behalf of all human beings but, again, through his divinity, he was resurrected, which signifies the renewed ability for human beings to come back into loving relationship with God and one another. This act wiped the slate clean and allows each of us the ability to choose good over evil and, further, allows us to grow in our relationship with God, which continually provides us with greater potential to live a life of perfected love towards God and one another. *THE GOSPEL.*

Remember, this is not to say that Christians are the only ones with the ability to choose the Good or that all who call themselves Christians always do good, but rather, it shows us that God, caring for all humanity, imparts to us the ability to choose good in the hopes that we will choose to enter into relationship with Him and perfect the goodness that He provides in our own lives.

So, the Christian worldview provides a logical foundation by which we are able to apprehend what is good, (whatever provides value to human beings, both individually and corporately, and fosters loving relationship between God and human beings and among humanity) and what is evil, (whatever devalues human beings, both individually and corporately, and hinders loving relationship between God and human beings and among humanity). It does so by asserting that a loving God who embodies and desires loving relationships created the universe and ordered reality in such a way that life lived according to these principles of morality is what is ultimately beneficial and satisfying for all. Such a view, because it is rooted in the very fabric of creation, is not subjective, but is objective and applicable to all. Also, because we are part of that creation, this view is rooted in our deepest selves. Further, God has provided the means by which we are able to overcome our selfish desires and develop our ability to choose actions and attitudes that reflect this reality. He sent Jesus Christ who, being fully human, showed us that a life of perfect love is possible and who, being fully God, sacrificed himself to bear witness to the penalties of sin and evil and bear those penalties on behalf of all humanity. Further, he was raised from the dead to show us that death is not the end, but that humanity was created for eternity and that we are part of the eternal kingdom (or eternal community) of God.

One wonders if, in the land of Hyrule, the Triforce of Wisdom (the transcendent force in Link's world) wasn't already calling out to Link as a young boy, not only pushing him to that fateful encounter with Zelda's nursemaid, but preparing him to choose to come to her aid, readying him to recognize the unjust use of power and, ultimately, equipping him from the very beginning to overcome the darkness of Ganon.

He steps through the broken entrance and lets his eyes adjust to the darkness. The familiar glare of the statues meets his gaze. He again crosses the threshold into the second room of the final dungeon. Link is somewhat disappointed to find the old man gone. His presence provided a modicum of comfort in this dark place. The reunited eight pieces of the Triforce glow briefly and the doors of the room rumble open. "Thank you, old one," Link thinks as he grips his sword tighter and unslings his shield, "I'm ready this time."

Author Biographies

Kyle Blanchette holds a Master's degree in theology from Asbury Theological Seminary and he is currently pursuing a Master's degree in philosophy from Western Michigan University. He is joyously married to his wife, Courtney. His favorite video game of all time is *Metal Gear Solid* and his favorite *Zelda* game is *A Link to the Past*.

D.M. Burke received his M.Div. from Asbury Theological Seminary and is currently residing in Fort Wayne, Indiana with his wife, two-year-old son and their dysfunctional dog, Chloe. His favorite video games include *The Legend of Zelda, Baldur's Gate II, Final Fantasy III, God of War I and II* and *Hitman: Blood Money.*

Josh A. Corman is an AP English Language and Composition teacher in his hometown of Nicholasville, Kentucky, where he routinely schools his students on the proper execution of compound-complex sentences and Link's Spin Attack in *Super Smash Brothers Melee*. He has supplemented his formal education (B.A. in English from the University of Kentucky, M.A. in English Education from Asbury University) with innumerable credit hours from the Nintendo School of Dungeon Crawling. His life's proudest moments are his marriage to his loving, patient wife, Sara, the birth of Benjamin, his wonderful son, and his completion of the Water Temple in *The Legend of Zelda: The Ocarina of Time.*

Benjamin B. DeVan has published numerous reviews and articles in venues like *Books & Culture, The Huffington Post, Journal for the Scientific Study of Religion, Women's Studies International Forum, Journal of Comparative Theology, Christian Apologetics Journal* and a book chapter on Martin Luther King, Jr. in *How to Get a Life: Empowering Wisdom for the Heart and Soul.* He has taught religion, philosophy and African American literature at North Carolina Central University, Peace

College and a January term mini-course at The Massachusetts Institute of Technology (MIT), "Religion: Bringing the World Together, or Tearing the World Apart?" DeVan earned his M.A. in Counseling at Asbury Seminary, his M.Div. at Duke University, a Th.M. in World Religions at Harvard University with a thesis on evangelical Christians and Muslims and is now a doctoral candidate at Durham University in Great Britain, writing a dissertation on the New Atheism. In his spare time, Ben tries to bring Thunder and Attack Power One to the Great Palace.

Dr. Mark Hayse is Professor of Christian Education in Olathe, Kansas. In 2009, he received the Ph.D. Educational Studies from Trinity International University in Deerfield, Illinois. His dissertation was entitled, "Religious Architecture in Videogames: Perspectives from Curriculum Theory and Religious Education." Recent publications in video game studies include "Ultima IV: Simulating the Religious Quest" in Halos and "Avatars: Playing Video Games with God" (2010 Westminster/John Knox) and several forthcoming entries in both The Concise Dictionary of Pop Culture and Theology (Westminster/John Knox) and the Encyclopedia of Video Games (Greenwood Press). His current research focuses upon the interplay of implicit curriculum, practical theology and procedural rhetoric in RPG, RTS and FPS video games. His favorite video games include *The Legend of Zelda: Wind Waker*; the *Ultima* series and the *Baldur's Gate* series. Mark and his wife, Karen, are the proud (and still quite young!) grandparents of three lovely granddaughters.

Justus Hunter is a Ph.D. student in the Graduate Program in Religious Studies at Southern Methodist University. As a child, he shared his *Legend of Zelda* adventures with his brother, John-Seth. Today, he shares them with his wife, Ellen.

Joshua Rasmussen, Ph.D. and his wife, **Rachel Rasmussen**, M.S. met at the University of Notre Dame where they got their advanced degrees. Josh is a research fellow at the University of Notre Dame, where he teaches classes on free will and the nature of minds. He has publications related to these topics in top philosophy journals (such as *Religious Studies* and *Philosophical Studies*) and presently is working on a book on the nature of truth. On their honeymoon, Josh and Rachel avidly played *Zelda: Twilight Princess*. Josh also enjoys video game programming and is teaming up with his wife to develop a game that he hopes to be even better than *Zelda*!

Rev. Jeremy Smith (@umjeremy) blames *Dune II* and *The Legend of Zelda: A Link to the Past* for his poor social standing in middle school. He persevered and received an M.Div. '06 from Boston University School of Theology. Jeremy is an ordained United Methodist minister and lives with his spouse and their two cats in rural Oklahoma. He blogs about faith, technology and Internet-age group theory at HackingChristianity.net

Philip Tallon is the author of "The Poetics of Evil: Toward an Aesthetic Theodicy" (forthcoming from Oxford University Press), as well as numerous essays on horror movies, comic books, fantasy novels and other pop culture products that have become gentrified of late. In 2009, he earned a Ph.D. in Theology from St. Andrews University.

Jonathan L. Walls lives in Los Angeles with his beautiful wife, Emily, and works in the film industry. He studied Media Communications with an emphasis on film at Asbury University. While his ambitions are to grow in the field of writing and directing films, he would love to one day write and direct a video game as well. His favorite games are *The Legend of Zelda: The Ocarina of Time*; *Resident Evil 4*; *The Legend of Zelda: The Windwaker*; *Bioshock* and *The Mass Effect series*. Also, he can school you in *Super Smash Brothers Melee*. He and his wife run a humor/opinion/pop culture website: Verbalinfusion.com.

Gray Matter Books

Gray Matter Books exists to promote discussion about matters of faith. Often the subjects we choose to explore represent gray areas where people of faith might have differing opinions. However, we believe that dialogue on these matters is healthy. Sharing ideas across idealistic lines and learning to respect each other betters us as people and believers. Gray Matter deeply values exploration that ranges from the intellectual to the popular culture, and especially how a person's faith is shaped by and continues to shape these areas.

Gray Matter Books
www.graymatterbooks.com

8033 Sunset Blvd. #164
Hollywood, CA. 90046